Hamlyn

FIRST

PICTURE
Dictionary

Contents

The First Picture Dictionary   page 4

Answers to the quizzes and puzzles   page 96

First published 1989 by The Hamlyn Publishing Group Limited,
Michelin House, 81 Fulham Road, London SW3 6RB, England.
Copyright © The Hamlyn Publishing Group Limited 1989
ISBN 0 600 56596 3

Printed in Great Britain

Illustrations by Peter Dennis, Gillian Hurry (Linda Rogers),
David Cook, Neil Harding (Linden Artists), Peter Bull, Gill
Tomblin, Oxford Illustrators, David Woodroffe,

Designed by Roger Walker/Linde Hardaker.
Cover Illustration by Julie Park.

Hamlyn

FIRST

PICTURE
Dictionary

Rosalind Fergusson

HAMLYN

above

Above means higher than. There is an aeroplane in the sky **above** the airport.

accident

An **accident** is something not done on purpose. I didn't mean to break the cup, it was an **accident**. There has been an **accident** outside the airport. A car has crashed into a van.

ache

When something **aches** it hurts for a long time. The noise of the traffic made my head **ache**.

aeroplane

door

uniform

newspaper

adults

baby

magazine

map

You can see aeroplanes at the airport.

a b c d e f g h i j k l m

act

When you **act** in a play, you pretend to be somebody else.

add

When you **add** numbers you find out how many there are altogether. If you **add** three and five, the answer is eight.

address

Your **address** tells people where you live.

adult

An **adult** is a grown-up person. Your father and your mother are **adults**.

adventure

An **adventure** is something exciting that happens. Our uncle told us about his **adventures** in the jungle.

advertisement

An **advertisement** tells you about something that you can buy. You see **advertisements** in newspapers and magazines and on television.

aeroplane

People travel through the air in an **aeroplane**. An **aeroplane** is sometimes called a plane.

afraid

My brother is **afraid** of horses. He doesn't like horses because he thinks that they might hurt him. Horses frighten him.

after

After tells you what comes next. Sunday is the day **after** Saturday. **After** tea we played in the garden.

afternoon

The **afternoon** is the part of the day between the morning and the evening. You usually come home from school in the **afternoon**.

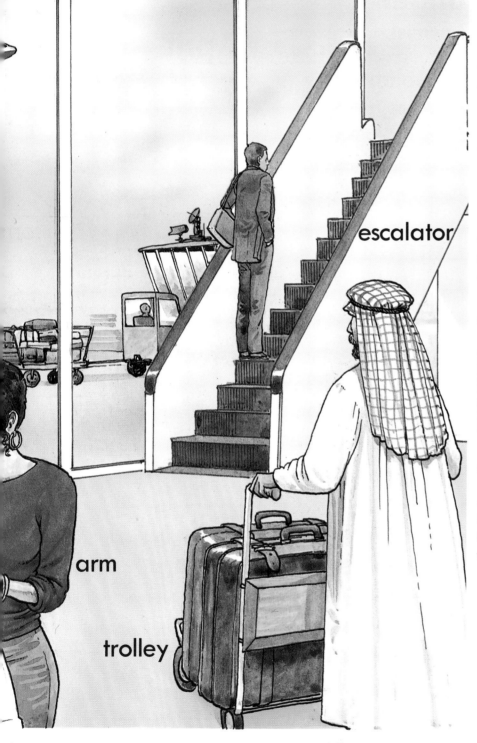

escalator

arm

trolley

age

Your **age** is how old you are.

agree

If you **agree** with somebody, you think the same. I think this is a good book. Do you **agree?**

aim

When you **aim**, you point at something that you want to hit. Sarah **aimed** her water pistol at her brother's head.

air

Air is all around you, but you cannot see it. We breathe **air**. You blow **air** into balloons.

airport

Aeroplanes take off and land at an **airport**.

alarm

An **alarm** is a noise that tells people about danger. We all left the building when we heard the fire **alarm**.

alive

Alive means not dead. Animals have to eat and breathe to stay **alive**.

allow

To **allow** is to let somebody do something. I am **allowed** to play football in the garden.

alphabet

The **alphabet** is the 26 different letters that we use to make words.

ambulance

An **ambulance** takes people to hospital.

angel

An **angel** is a messenger from God. **Angels** have wings.

angry

The teacher was **angry** with the naughty boy. My father was **angry** because I forgot to post his letter.

animal

An **animal** is a living thing. Dogs, horses, monkeys and elephants are all **animals**. Birds, fish, insects, and people are also **animals**.

ankle

Your foot is joined to your leg at your **ankle**.

answer

You get an **answer** when you ask a question. What colour is a banana? The **answer** is yellow.

ant

An **ant** is a very small insect that crawls on the ground.

apple

An **apple** is a fruit that you can eat. **Apples** grow on trees.

April

April is the fourth month of the year. **April** comes after March and before May.

apron

You wear an **apron** to keep your clothes clean when you are cooking.

area

The **area** is the size of something flat. Let's measure the **area** of the floor to find out how much carpet we need.

argue

If you **argue** with somebody, you do not agree. The children **argued** about the rules of the game.

arm

Your **arm** is the part of your body between your shoulder and your hand.

a b c d e f g h i j k l m

around

The dog has a collar **around** its neck. An island has water all **around** it.

arrest

The police **arrest** people who have done something wrong. They **arrested** the burglars and put them in prison.

arrow

An **arrow** is a pointed stick shot from a bow.

An **arrow** is also a sign that shows you which way to go.

ask

You **ask** a question. My teacher **asked** me what I was doing. You can also **ask** somebody to do something. I **asked** Kit to open a window.

asleep

Asleep means sleeping. The baby is **asleep**. Don't make a noise and wake her up.

astronaut

An **astronaut** is a person who travels in space. Some **astronauts** have walked on the moon.

ALPHABET

Here are the 26 letters of the alphabet:
a b c d e f g h i j k l m n o p q r s t u v w x y z
They are in **alphabetical order**, with the letter **a** at the beginning and the letter **z** at the end.

In alphabetical order, the letter **m** comes after the letter **d** and before the letter **t**. These letters are in alphabetical order:
b e h l r u.

The words in this dictionary are in alphabetical order. That means that the words beginning with the letter **a** are at the beginning and the words beginning with the letter **z** are at the end. The word **mouse** comes a long way after the word **dog** and a long way before the word **tiger**. These words are in alphabetical order:
bat egg house letter road umbrella.

Can you put the words in this box in alphabetical order?

time kettle fire sand apple wet

When two words begin with the same letter, we have to look at the second letter to put them in alphabetical order. The word **brown** comes after the word **blue** because the letter **r** comes after the letter **l**. These words are in alphabetical order:
cat ceiling chair clock comb cup.

Can you put the words in this box in alphabetical order?

sky stool smile shoe sit swim

Answers on page 96

attack

To **attack** is to start fighting. The army **attacked** the town.

August

August is the eighth month of the year. **August** comes after July and before September.

aunt

Your **aunt** is your mother's sister or your father's sister.

autumn

Autumn is the season between summer and winter. In **autumn** the leaves fall from the trees.

awake

Awake means not sleeping. Is the baby **awake**?

axe

An **axe** is a sharp tool that is used to cut down trees and to chop wood.

n o p q r s t u v w x y z

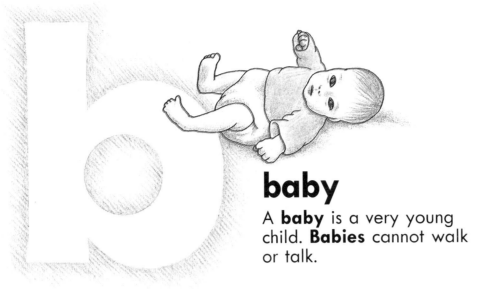

baby

A **baby** is a very young child. **Babies** cannot walk or talk.

back

Back is the opposite of front. We sat at the **back** of the hall.

Your **back** is the part of your body that is behind you, between your neck and your bottom.

sail

boat

sandwich

box

basket

umbrel

8

On the beach

a **b** c d e f g h i j k l m

bad

Bad means not good. We had very **bad** weather on our holidays. It rained every day.

badge

A **badge** is pinned or sewn on your clothes. I wear a **badge** to show that I belong to the swimming club.

bag

You put things in a **bag** to carry them or to keep them together. He carried his grandmother's heavy

shopping **bag**. She gave him a **bag** of sweets.

bake

You **bake** food in an oven. The cook has **baked** some bread and cakes.

balance

To **balance** is to keep steady without falling. Can you **balance** on one leg?

bald

A **bald** man has no hair on his head.

ball

A **ball** is round. You play lots of games with a **ball**. The children on the beach are playing with a **ball**.

ballet

Ballet is a kind of dance. My sister goes to **ballet** classes.

balloon

You blow up a **balloon** to fill it with air. **Balloons** are very light. We had lots of coloured **balloons** at our party.

boy

sand

spade

bucket

beach

net

bird

rock

crab

banana

A **banana** is a long fruit with a yellow skin. You can peel the skin off the **banana** and eat the fruit inside.

bandage

A **bandage** is a long strip of white cloth. You wrap a **bandage** around a cut finger or leg.

bank

A **bank** is a place where money is kept.

A **bank** is also the side of a river. The fisherman was sitting on the **bank**.

basket

A **basket** is made of sticks or straw. You can put things in a **basket** to carry them or to keep them together.

bat

You use a **bat** to hit a ball. The children on the beach are playing with a **bat** and ball.

A **bat** is also an animal that flies at night.

bath

When you have a **bath** you wash your whole body. I like playing with my toy boats in the **bath**.

beach

The **beach** is the land by the sea. The **beach** is covered with sand. What else can you see on the **beach**?

beak

A **beak** is part of a bird's mouth. It is hard and pointed. The parrot has a curved **beak**.

bear

A **bear** is a large wild animal that is covered with fur. You can see **bears** at the zoo.

beard

A **beard** is the hair that grows on a man's chin.

beat

If you **beat** somebody in a race, you run faster. When you win a football match you **beat** the other team.

because

Because tells us why. You can't play outside **because** it is raining.

bed

You sleep in a **bed** at night. What time do you go to **bed**?

before

Before tells you what comes first. Saturday is the day **before** Sunday. Look both ways **before** you cross the road.

begin

To **begin** is to do the first part of something. I will not **begin** the story until everybody is quiet. It is **beginning** to snow.

behave

When you **behave** yourself, you are not naughty. All the children **behaved** very well at the party.

believe

If you **believe** something, you think it is true. My mother told me that it was raining, but I didn't **believe** her. Do you **believe** in fairies?

bell

A **bell** rings when you shake it or when you press it. Rachel rang the **bell**, but nobody came to open the door.

belong

This pen **belongs** to me. It is my pen.

a **b** c d e f g h i j k l m

below

Below means lower than. The windows of this house are **below** the roof.

belt

A **belt** is a strip of leather or plastic that you wear around your waist.

bend

When something **bends**, it is not straight. Can you **bend** this stick without breaking it? The tall man had to **bend** down to talk to the little girl.

between

Between means in the middle. Wednesday comes **between** Tuesday and Thursday. Michael is standing **between** his two sisters.

bicycle

A **bicycle** has two wheels. Can you ride a **bicycle**? A **bicycle** is sometimes called a bike.

big

Big is the opposite of little. An elephant is a **big** animal.

bird

A **bird** has wings and feathers. Most **birds** can fly.

birthday

Today is my brother's sixth **birthday**. He was born six years ago. He is having a **birthday** party.

biscuit

A **biscuit** is flat and crisp. **Biscuits** are nice to eat.

bite

When you **bite** something, you cut it with your teeth. Do not touch zoo animals or they might **bite** you.

black

Black is the colour of coal. Here is a **black** cat.

blanket

A **blanket** is a cover that you put on a bed. **Blankets** keep you warm.

blood

Blood is the red liquid that you see when you cut yourself. The **blood** inside your body helps to keep you alive.

blow

To **blow** is to make the air move. The wind is **blowing** the leaves all over the garden. Can you **blow** out all the candles on your birthday cake?

blue

Blue is the colour of the sky on a sunny day. Here is a **blue** ball.

n o p q r s t u v w x y z

boat

You travel in a **boat** on water.

body

Your **body** is the whole of you, from your head to your feet. A cat has fur all over its **body**.

boil

Water **boils** when it is very hot. **Boiling** water makes bubbles and steam.

bomb

A **bomb** explodes with a very loud noise. The soldiers used a **bomb** to blow up the building.

bone

A **bone** is a hard part of an animal's body. You have lots of **bones** inside your body.

book

A **book** has pages. You can read a **book** that has words and pictures.

borrow

Can I **borrow** your crayons? I'll give them back when I've finished colouring my picture.

bottle

A **bottle** is made of glass or plastic. It has a narrow part at the top. We bought a **bottle** of lemonade at the supermarket.

bottom

The **bottom** is the lowest part of something. The stone sank to the **bottom** of the pond.

Your **bottom** is the part of your body that you sit on.

bounce

To **bounce** is to spring back. He threw the ball against the wall and it **bounced** back. The children **bounced** up and down on their beds.

bow

A **bow** is a knot with two loops. You can tie a **bow** in a ribbon or in a shoelace.

A **bow** is also a curved stick that is used to shoot arrows.

bowl

A **bowl** is a deep round dish. You can eat soup out of a **bowl**. Some people keep fruit in a **bowl**.

box

You can keep things in a **box**. **Boxes** are usually made of cardboard or wood.

boy

A **boy** is a male child. When a **boy** grows up he becomes a man.

brave

A **brave** person is not frightened. The **brave** woman dived into the water to rescue the puppy.

bread

You use **bread** to make sandwiches or toast. **Bread** is baked in an oven.

break

When you **break** something, it falls into pieces. Be careful with that glass bowl, it will **break** if you drop it.

breakfast

Breakfast is the first meal of the day. We eat **breakfast** in the morning. What do you have for **breakfast**?

breathe

To **breathe** is to take air in and out of your body. You usually **breathe**

a **b** c d e f g h i j k l m

through your nose. All animals have to **breathe** to stay alive.

brick

A **brick** is a hard block that is used to build a wall. Most houses are built of **bricks**.

bridge

You go across a **bridge** over a river, a road, or a railway.

bring

When you **bring** something, you take it with you. Don't forget to **bring** your gym shoes to school tomorrow.

brother

Mr and Mrs Smith have two children, Jane and Paul. Paul is Jane's **brother**. Do you have a **brother**?

brown

Brown is the colour of chocolate. Here is a **brown** rabbit.

bruise

A **bruise** is a purple patch under your skin. I had a big **bruise** on my knee after I fell down the steps.

brush

You use a **brush** to keep things clean and tidy. You sweep the floor with a **brush**. You **brush** your hair with a different kind of **brush**.

bubble

A **bubble** is small and round and full of air. There are **bubbles** in fizzy lemonade.

bucket

We carry water in a **bucket**.

build

To **build** is to make something by putting parts together. My father is going to **build** a shed in the garden.

bulb

Some plants grow from **bulbs**. The **bulb** is the round part that is under the ground.

There is a different kind of **bulb** inside an electric light. These **bulbs** are also round. They are made of glass.

bull

A **bull** is a large male animal that is like a cow. **Bulls** have horns. You can see a **bull** on a farm.

burn

Things **burn** when they are very hot. Let's **burn** this paper on the fire. If the oven is too hot, the cake will **burn**.

bus

A **bus** carries lots of people along the road. Some children travel to school on a **bus**.

busy

A **busy** person has lots of things to do. My mother has been **busy** in the garden all afternoon.

butterfly

A **butterfly** is an insect with coloured wings.

button

A **button** is small and round. **Buttons** are used to fasten coats and shirts.

buy

When you **buy** something, you pay money for it. I went to the baker's shop to **buy** some bread.

n o p q r s t u v w x y z

cage

Some animals are kept in **cages**. A **cage** has metal bars to stop the animals from escaping.

cake

A **cake** is sweet and nice to eat. Some **cakes** have icing on the top.

calendar

A **calendar** shows us the days and months of the year. There is a **calendar** hanging on the wall.

camel

A **camel** is a large animal with a hump on its back. **Camels** live in the desert.

camera

You use a **camera** to take photographs.

candle

A **candle** is a stick of wax that you can light with a flame. My sister had eight **candles** on her birthday cake.

capital

A, B, C, and D are **capital** letters. We use a **capital** letter at the beginning of a sentence. Your name also begins with a **capital** letter.

car

A **car** has wheels and an engine to make it move. You can travel on the road in a **car**.

caravan

A **caravan** is like a house on wheels. You can tow a **caravan** behind a car.

card

A **card** is a stiff piece of paper. A birthday **card** has a picture on the front and writing inside. You can play games with playing **cards**.

cardboard

Cardboard is very stiff paper. **Cardboard** is used to make boxes.

carpet

A **carpet** covers the floor. A **carpet** is soft to walk on.

carrot

A **carrot** is a long orange vegetable. You can eat **carrots** raw or cooked.

carry

When you **carry** something, you pick it up and take it somewhere. He **carried** the heavy box into the kitchen.

cartoon

A **cartoon** is a funny drawing or film. You see **cartoons** on television and in comics. I like Bugs Bunny **cartoons**.

a b c d e f g h i j k l m

castle

A **castle** is a large building where kings and queens used to live. **Castles** have very strong walls.

cat

A **cat** is an animal that is covered with fur. Some people keep **cats** at home as pets.

catch

My friend threw the ball and I tried to **catch** it in my hands. If you **catch** a cold, you get it from somebody else.

caterpillar

A **caterpillar** looks like a short coloured worm. A **caterpillar** changes into a butterfly.

ceiling

The **ceiling** is the flat top of a room. My uncle is so tall, his head nearly touches the **ceiling**.

chair

You sit on a **chair**. A **chair** has four legs and a back. Some **chairs** have arms.

change

To **change** is to become different. I don't like my name, I wish I could **change** it. When you **change** your clothes, you put on different clothes.

chase

To **chase** means to run after. Jennifer **chased** the dog down the street, but she couldn't catch it.

cheap

Something that is **cheap** does not cost very much money. **Cheap** is the opposite of expensive.

check

To **check** is to make sure. I went back into the room to **check** that I had switched the television off.

cheek

Your **cheek** is the soft part of your face beside your nose and mouth. Your **cheeks** turn red when you blush.

cheese sandwiches for my lunch today.

chest

Your **chest** is the front part of your body between your neck and your waist. Your **chest** moves when you breathe.

A **chest** is also a big strong box.

child

A **child** is a young person. Boys and girls are **children**.

chimney

Smoke goes up through a **chimney**. Some houses and factories have **chimneys**.

chin

Your **chin** is the hard part of your face below your mouth.

chocolate

Chocolate is brown and sweet and nice to eat. My uncle bought me a bar of **chocolate**.

choose

When you **choose** something, you pick it out because it is the one you want. There are so many books it will take me a long time to **choose** one.

chain

A **chain** is a row of metal rings joined together.

cheese

Cheese is a food that is made from milk. I had

n o p q r s t u v w x y z

Christmas

At **Christmas** people remember the birth of Jesus Christ. They give **Christmas** presents and decorate **Christmas** trees. They send **Christmas** cards. **Christmas** Day is 25th December.

church

A **church** is a building where people meet to sing hymns and to pray to God.

circle

A **circle** is a round shape.

circus

A **circus** is a show that takes place in a big tent. You can see clowns at the **circus**.

city

A **city** is a very large and

hat

arm

ear

egg

Christmas presents

card

tea

envelop

Christmas shopping

a b **c** d e f g h i j k l m

important town. Do you live in a **city**?

clap

When you **clap**, you hit your hands together to make a noise. We all **clapped** at the end of the show.

claw

A **claw** is a hard pointed nail on an animal's foot. The cat scratched the door with her **claws**.

clean

When you wash

something, you make it **clean**. **Clean** means not dirty.

clear

You can see through something that is **clear**. The water was so **clear**, we could see right to the bottom of the lake.

clever

A **clever** person learns quickly and knows a lot of things.

climb

When you **climb**, you go up something using your hands and feet. The children are **climbing** the tree.

beard

Christmas tree

sausage

elephant

17

n o p q r s t u v w x y z

clock

A **clock** shows us the time. What is the time on this **clock**?

close

To **close** is to shut. **Close** the window, it's cold in here.

Close means near. Don't sit too **close** to the fire.

clothes

Clothes are things that you wear. Dresses, trousers, shirts and jumpers are all **clothes**.

cloud

You see **clouds** in the sky. **Clouds** are white or grey. Dark grey **clouds** bring rain.

clown

A **clown** is a person who does funny things to make us laugh. **Clowns** usually dress up in silly clothes and paint their faces.

club

A **club** is a group of people who meet together. I joined the art **club** because I like painting and drawing.

coach

A **coach** is a bus that carries people a long way.

coat

You wear a **coat** when you go outside on a cold day. A **coat** goes on top of your other clothes.

coffee

Coffee is a hot brown drink.

coin

A **coin** is a piece of money. **Coins** are made of metal.

cold

Cold is the opposite of hot. Ice cream and snow are **cold**. My hands were **cold**, so I put my gloves on.

collar

A **collar** is part of a piece of clothing. The **collar** goes around your neck. This shirt has a white **collar**.

A **collar** is also a thin band that goes around a dog's neck.

collect

When you **collect** things, you get a lot of them and keep them together. My cousin **collects** postcards.

colour

The **colour** of grass is green. Red, blue, yellow, orange and purple are **colours**.

comb

You use a **comb** to keep your hair tidy. I always **comb** my hair before I go out.

comic

A **comic** has funny stories and pictures in it. My sister bought a **comic** to read on the train.

computer

A **computer** is a machine that keeps information and works out answers.

cook

You **cook** food to make it hot and ready to eat. We **cooked** sausages on the barbecue.

copy

To **copy** is to do exactly the same. The teacher drew a picture on the board and we all **copied** it.

a b **c** d e f g h i j k l m

corner

A **corner** is the place where two lines or two sides meet. There is a bird cage in the **corner** of the room.

cost

What does this toy **cost**? How much money do I need to buy it? It **costs** two pounds.

costume

You wear a **costume** when you dress up as somebody else. I wore a rabbit **costume** in the school play.

cough

When you **cough**, you make a rough croaking sound. My friend can't come to the party because she has a bad **cough**.

count

You **count** things to find out how many there are. Can you **count** to a hundred? One, two, three, four, ...

country

The world is divided into **countries**. France is a **country**. Which **country** do you live in?

cousin

Your **cousin** is the child of your aunt and uncle.

cover

To **cover** is to put one thing on top of another. The ground was **covered** with snow. We **covered** the table with a cloth.

cow

A **cow** is an animal that gives milk. You can see **cows** on a farm.

crab

A **crab** is an animal with a hard shell and ten legs. **Crabs** live by the sea, you sometimes find them on the beach.

crane

A **crane** is a tall machine that is used to lift heavy things.

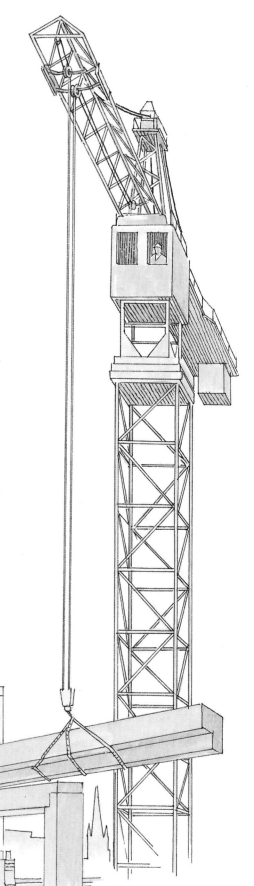

crawl

Babies **crawl** along on their hands and knees before they learn to walk.

crayon

You can use **crayons** to colour a picture. Colour the sky with a blue **crayon**.

cross

When we **cross** the road, we go from one side to the other.

A **cross** is a sign like the letter X.

A **cross** person is not pleased. My mother will be **cross** when she sees our muddy footprints on her clean floor.

crowd

A **crowd** is a lot of people together in the same place.

crown

A **crown** is a large ring that you wear on your head. Kings and queens sometimes wear a **crown**.

cruel

A **cruel** person hurts other people or animals. It is **cruel** to pull a cat's tail.

crumb

A **crumb** is a very small piece of food. Your greedy brother has eaten all the biscuits, there are only a few **crumbs** left.

cry

We **cry** when we are sad or in pain. When you **cry**, tears come out of your eyes. Jonathan **cried** because he had hurt his knee.

cup

You drink from a **cup**. A **cup** has a handle.

cupboard

A **cupboard** is a piece of furniture with shelves. You can keep things in a **cupboard**.

curl

A **curl** is a piece of hair that is not straight. Elizabeth has **curls**.

spelling tip

The letter **c** has three different sounds. It sounds like the letter **k** in these words: **candle cold picture uncle**.
It sounds like the letter **s** in these words: **ceiling city juice race**.

When the letter **c** comes before the letter **h** it makes another sound: **chair cheek sandwich lunch**.

curtain

Curtains hang at the sides of a window. At night we pull the **curtains** across the window to cover it.

cushion

A **cushion** is a soft pad that makes a chair more comfortable. There are two **cushions** on the sofa.

cut

You **cut** things with a knife or with scissors. **Cut** the cake into four pieces.

a b c d e f g h i j k l m

dance

When you **dance**, you move your body to the sound of music.

dangerous

Something that is **dangerous** can hurt you. It is **dangerous** to play with matches.

dark

There is no light in a **dark** place. It is **dark** at night.

date

The **date** tells us the day, month and year. The **date** of my birthday is 29th May. What is today's **date**?

daughter

A girl is the **daughter** of her father and mother.

day

The **day** is the time when it is light outside.
    There are seven **days** in a week: Monday, Tuesday, Wednesday, Thursday, Friday, Saturday and Sunday.

dead

When an animal or plant dies, it is **dead**. My grandfather is **dead**, he was killed in the war.

deaf

A **deaf** person cannot hear.

dear

We put the word **dear** before somebody's name when we are writing a letter.
    Dear also means expensive.

December

December is the last month of the year. **December** comes after November.

decide

To **decide** is to make up your mind. Catherine **decided** to wear her blue dress for the party.

deck

On a boat or ship, the **deck** is the flat part that you can walk on.

deep

Deep means that it is a long way down to the bottom. The water under the diving board is very **deep**.

dentist

A **dentist** looks after your teeth.

desert

A **desert** is a very hot place that is covered with sand. There is not much water in the **desert**.

desk

A **desk** is a kind of table. You sit at a **desk** to write or draw.

dice

Dice are small cubes with a different number of spots on each side. In some games you have to throw the **dice** to see how far along the board you can move. One dice is called a **die**.

dictionary

A **dictionary** is a book that shows us how to spell words and tells us what they mean. This book is a **dictionary**.

die

To **die** is to stop living. Many plants **die** in the winter.

different

Different means not the same. My T-shirt is not like my friend's T-shirt, it is **different**.

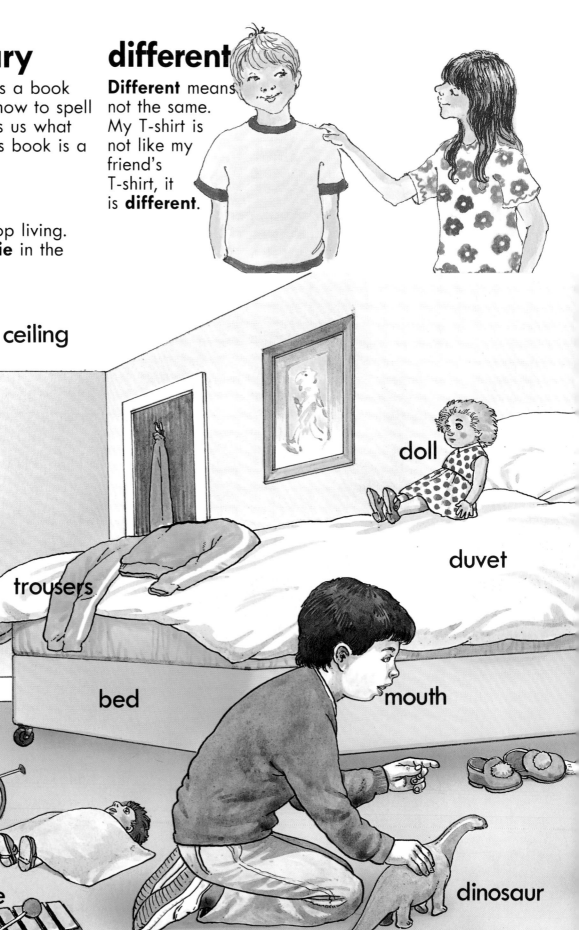

ceiling

doll

duvet

trousers

bed

mouth

bow

xylophone

dinosaur

The children are playing with toy dinosaurs.

22

a b c **d** e f g h i j k l m

dig

To **dig** is to make a hole with a spade. You can **dig** in the sand on the beach. You can also **dig** in the garden.

dinner

Dinner is the main meal of the day. Some people eat their **dinner** in the middle of the day, some eat it in the evening.

dinosaur

A **dinosaur** is a large animal that lived on the earth millions of years ago. The children in the bedroom are playing with toy **dinosaurs**.

dirty

My shoes are **dirty** because I have been walking in the mud. You wash **dirty** things to make them clean.

disappear

If something **disappears**, you cannot see it any more. When you switch the television off, the picture **disappears**.

disguise

You **disguise** yourself to make yourself look different. My sister **disguised** herself as an old lady.

disturb

When you **disturb** somebody, you make a noise or ask a question and stop a person doing something. Don't **disturb** the baby, she's sleeping. Don't wake her up.

dive

To **dive** is to jump into water headfirst. The swimmer **dived** into the pool.

doctor

A **doctor** looks after people who are ill and helps them to get better.

illow
light
ose
drum
wrist
toys

23

dog

A **dog** is an animal that barks. Some people keep **dogs** at home as pets.

doll

A **doll** is a toy that looks like a baby or a person.

door

You open a **door** to go in or out. The **door** of the bedroom is closed.

dot

A **dot** is a very small round spot. Here is a row of **dots**.

. . . .

double

Double means two or twice. I had a **double** helping of chips with my hamburger.

dragon

A **dragon** is an animal that can breathe fire through its nose. You read about **dragons** in stories, but there are no real **dragons**.

draw

When you **draw** a picture, you make lines on a piece of paper.

drawer

A **drawer** is an open box that slides in and out of a piece of furniture. You can keep things in a **drawer**.

dream

We **dream** when we are asleep. Last night I had a **dream** about swimming in a sea of chocolate.

dress

A **dress** is a piece of clothing that girls and women wear.
    To **dress** is to put your clothes on. I always get **dressed** before breakfast.

drill

A **drill** is a tool that is used for making holes.

drink

To **drink** is to swallow liquid. Please may I have a **drink** of water?

drive

To **drive** a car is to make it go along the road. My father **drives** to work every day.

drop

When you **drop** something, you let it fall. I **dropped** my pen on the floor.

drown

To **drown** is to die in water. People **drown** because they breathe water instead of air.

drum

A **drum** is a musical instrument. You play a **drum** by hitting it.

dry

Dry means not wet. Is the paint **dry** yet? Wash your hands and **dry** them on this towel.

dust

Dust is powder that floats in the air and lands on things. The shelves are covered with **dust**.

duvet

A **duvet** is a thick warm cover that you put on a bed.

a b c **d** e f g h i j k l m

ear

You have two **ears**, one on each side of your head. We hear with our **ears**.

early

The bus was **early** this morning. It usually comes at half past eight, but today it came at quarter past eight.

earth

Our world is called the **earth**. The **earth** is a long way from the sun.

easy

Something that is **easy** is not hard to do. Everybody knows the answer to an **easy** question.

eat

When we **eat** food, we bite it and swallow it. Are you going to **eat** all those biscuits?

echo

You sometimes hear an **echo** when you shout in a cave or in a tunnel. The sound bounces off the walls and you hear it again and again.

edge

The **edge** is the side or the end of something. The glass is near the **edge** of the table.

egg

Hens lay **eggs** for us to eat. Baby birds grow inside **eggs**.

eight

Eight is the number that comes after seven. Here are **eight** cars.

elastic

You can stretch **elastic**. My socks have **elastic** at the top.

elbow

Your **elbow** is the place where your arm bends.

electricity

Electricity is a power that makes machines work.

elephant

An **elephant** is a very big animal with sharp tusks and a long trunk.

eleven

Eleven is the number that comes after ten. Here are **eleven** stars.

empty

Empty is the opposite of full. There is nothing inside an **empty** box.

spelling tip

When the letter **e** comes at the end of a word, it is usually a silent letter. You do not say the letter **e** in these words: **table glove bridge**. The letter **e** sometimes changes the sound of another letter in the word:

The letter **a** sounds different in the words **hat** and **hate**. The letter **i** sounds different in the words **lid** and **ride**. The letter **o** sounds different in the words **hop** and **hope**. The letter **u** sounds different in the words **sun** and **tune**.

end

The **end** is the last part of something. Your hand is at the **end** of your arm.

engine

An **engine** is a machine that makes things work. The **engine** in a car makes the car go.

enjoy

To **enjoy** is to have fun doing something. I **enjoy** playing on the swings in the park.

enormous

Enormous means very big.

enough

Enough is as much as you need. I have **enough** money to buy an ice cream.

envelope

You put a letter in an **envelope** before you post it. You write the address on the **envelope**.

squirrel

shop

fountain

seats

swings

seesaw

slide

green grass

In the park

a b c d e f g h i j k l m

equal

Equal means the same. Two and three **equals** five.

escalator

An **escalator** has stairs that move up or down.

escape

To **escape** is to get away.

A lion has **escaped** from the zoo.

evening

The **evening** is the last part of the day. You usually go to bed in the **evening**.

exercise

An **exercise** is a piece of work that helps you to learn. Another kind of **exercise** helps you to keep fit. The children are doing their **exercises**.

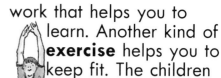

exit

The **exit** is the way out of a room or a building.

expect

If you **expect** something, you think it will happen. I **expect** it will rain this afternoon.

expensive

Something that is **expensive** costs a lot of money. **Expensive** is the opposite of cheap.

explain

To **explain** is to help somebody understand. Can you **explain** to me how a computer works?

explode

To **explode** is to blow up. The bomb **exploded** with a loud bang.

explore

When you **explore** a place, you look around it for the first time. We set off to **explore** the castle.

eye

You have two **eyes** on your face. We see with our **eyes**.

sky

steps

sock

shoe

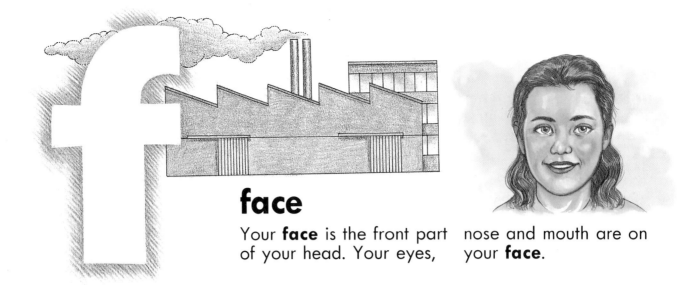

face

Your **face** is the front part of your head. Your eyes, nose and mouth are on your **face**.

sheep

lamb

fiel

fence

pig

horse

goose

fac

hen

On the farm

a b c d e **f** g h i j k l m

factory

A **factory** is a place where things are made. My uncle works in a car **factory**.

fair

A **fair** has lots of things for you to play and ride on. I like going on the big wheel at the **fair**.

Something that is **fair** seems right. It's not **fair**, you gave Mark four sweets but you gave me only two.

Fair is a light colour. Lisa has **fair** hair.

fairy

A **fairy** is a little person that you read about in stories. **Fairies** can do magic things.

cow

tractor

farmer

finger

flowers

fruit

goat

fall

When you **fall**, you go down to the ground. In autumn the leaves **fall** from the trees.

false

False means not true or not real.

family

A **family** is a mother and a father and their children. How many people are there in your **family**?

famous

Famous means well-known. You often see **famous** people on television.

far

Far means a long way. I can't read the sign, it's too **far** away. Is it **far** to the station from here?

farm

A **farm** is a place where food is grown and animals are kept.

farmer

A **farmer** is a person who has a farm.

fast

Fast means quickly. The dog ran so **fast**, I couldn't catch him.

fat

A **fat** person is wide and heavy. If you eat too many cakes and sweets you will get **fat**. **Fat** is the opposite of thin.

father

Your **father** is the man in your family. Mr Jones has a child called Elizabeth. Mr Jones is Elizabeth's **father**.

fault

Fault tells us who is to blame. I didn't break the window, it's not my **fault**. It's your own **fault** that your hands are cold, I told you to wear your gloves.

favourite

Your **favourite** is the one that you like best. What is your **favourite** colour?

feast

A **feast** is a special meal with many nice things to eat and drink. We bought cakes and lemonade for our midnight **feast**.

feather

A bird has **feathers** all over its body. **Feathers** are very light.

February

February is the second month of the year. **February** comes after January and before March.

feed

When you **feed** a baby or an animal you give it food.

feel

To **feel** is to be or to seem. The good news made me **feel** very happy. It **feels** cold outside.

    Feel also means touch. She bent down to **feel** the smooth rock.

fence

A **fence** is a kind of wall made of wood or metal. There is a **fence** around the field to keep the sheep in.

few

Few means not many. There are a **few** sweets left in the jar.

field

A **field** is a piece of land. A **field** is covered with grass or other plants.

fight

When you **fight** you try to hurt somebody because you are angry. My friend had a **fight** with her brother.

fill

To **fill** is to put as much as you can into something. I **filled** the bucket with water.

film

You go to the cinema to see a **film**. You sometimes see **films** on television.

    A **film** is also a strip of plastic that we put in a camera to take photographs.

find

You **find** something that has been lost. I've looked in all my pockets, but I can't **find** my key.

finger

Our **fingers** are at the ends of our hands. We have four **fingers** and a thumb on each hand.

finish

To **finish** means to come to the end. Have you **finished** your story?

fire

Fire is the hot, bright light that comes when things burn.

first

First means at the front or at the beginning. If you win a race, you come **first**. We start reading on the **first** page of a book.

fish

A **fish** is an animal that lives in water.

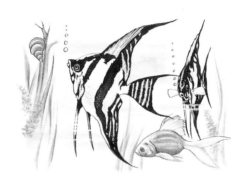

fit

To **fit** is to be the right size. These shoes don't **fit** me, they are too small.

Fit also means healthy and not ill.

five

Five is the number that comes after four. Here are **five** flowers.

flag

A **flag** is a coloured piece of cloth at the end of a stick. Every country has its own **flag**.

flame

A **flame** is the part of fire that you see. There is a **flame** at the top of a lit candle.

flat

Flat means smooth and level. A **flat** surface has no lumps in it. A **flat** roof is not sloping.

flavour

The **flavour** of something is what it tastes of. Which **flavour** of ice cream do you want, strawberry or chocolate?

float

When something **floats**, it does not sink or fall. Boats **float** on the water. Balloons **float** in the air.

flood

A **flood** is a lot of water. The heavy rain **flooded** the town, the streets were full of water.

floor

A **floor** is the flat bottom of a room. People walk on the **floor**.

flour

Flour is white powder. You can make bread and cakes with **flour**.

flower

A **flower** is the coloured part of a plant.

fly

To **fly** is to travel through the air. Birds and aeroplanes **fly**.

A **fly** is a small insect with wings.

fog

Fog is a thick cloud in the air around us. You cannot see very far in the **fog**.

fold

When you **fold** something, you bend one part over another. I **folded** the letter so that it would fit in the envelope.

follow

To **follow** is to go after. **Follow** me, I'll show you the way.

food

Food is everything that you eat. We eat **food** to stay alive.

foot

Your **foot** is at the end of your leg. We have two **feet**.

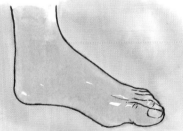

forehead

Your **forehead** is the part of your face that is above your eyes.

forest

In a **forest** there are a lot of trees growing close together.

forget

If you **forget** something, you do not remember it. My grandmother always **forgets** my birthday. Don't **forget** to lock the door.

fork

We use a **fork** to pick up food. A **fork** has points at the end.

a b c d e **f** g h i j k l m

fountain

Water sprays up into the air in a **fountain**. There is a **fountain** in the park.

four

Four is the number that comes after three. Here are **four** eggs.

free

You do not have to pay for something that is **free**. There is a **free** toy inside this packet of cornflakes.

When you are **free**, you can go anywhere and do anything. They set the prisoner **free**.

freeze

Things **freeze** when they become very cold. When water **freezes**, it turns into ice.

Friday

Friday is one of the days of the week. **Friday** comes after Thursday and before Saturday.

friend

Friends like each other and often do things together. I play with my **friends** after school.

frighten

To **frighten** is to make someone feel afraid. My sister jumped out from behind the wall and **frightened** me.

frog

A **frog** is an animal that lives near water. **Frogs** have strong legs for jumping.

front

The **front** is the first part of something. The **front** of a house faces forwards. **Front** is the opposite of back.

frost

Frost is a thin white layer of ice. On a very cold day you sometimes see **frost** on the ground and on trees and houses.

frown

People **frown** when they are worried or puzzled or sad or angry. When you **frown**, you wrinkle your forehead.

fruit

Apples, bananas, oranges and grapes are **fruit**. **Fruit** grows on bushes and trees. **Fruit** contains the seeds of a plant.

fry

To **fry** is to cook food in hot fat or oil.

full

When something is **full**, there is no space to put anything else inside it. The bucket is **full** of water.

fun

If you are having **fun**, you like what you are doing. The children had **fun** at the party.

funny

Something that is **funny** makes us laugh.

fur

Fur is the short soft hairs that a cat has all over its body. Many other animals have **fur**.

furniture

Chairs, tables, beds and cupboards are all **furniture**.

future

The **future** is the time that has not happened yet. Tomorrow and next year are in the **future**.

gallop

A horse **gallops** when it runs fast.

game

A **game** is something that you play. **Games** are fun. Let's have a **game** of hide and seek.

garage

A **garage** is a building where you can keep a car. A **garage** is also a place where cars are mended.

garden

A **garden** is a piece of land where you can grow

ladder

window

garage

car

gloves

gnome

pa

goldfish

In the garden

a b c d e f g h i j k l m

flowers and vegetables. We played in the **garden** all afternoon.

gas

Gas is burned to give heat for cooking and to make the house warm. You cannot see **gas**.

gate

A **gate** is a kind of door in a wall or in a fence.

ghost

A **ghost** is the spirit of a dead person. The man told me that the castle was haunted by a **ghost**, but I didn't believe him.

giant

A **giant** is a very big person that you read about in stories. There are no real **giants**.

giraffe

A **giraffe** is an animal with a very long neck. You can see **giraffes** at the zoo.

girl

A **girl** is a female child. When a **girl** grows up she becomes a woman.

give

To **give** is to let another person have something. My brother always **gives** me some of his sweets.

glass

Windows are made of **glass**. **Glass** is hard and you can see through it.

A **glass** is a kind of cup without a handle. It is made of **glass** and you can drink from it.

glasses

People wear **glasses** in front of their eyes to help them see better. The man in the garden is wearing **glasses**.

glove

We wear **gloves** on our hands to keep them warm and dry.

greenhouse

wave

garden

girl

The letter **g** has two different sounds. You can hear one of these sounds if you read these words aloud: **gate green pig begin**. You can hear the other sound if you read these words aloud: **giant gymnastics** cage engine.

The letters **gh** are found together in many words. Sometimes they make a sound like the letter **f**: **cough laugh rough enough**. Sometimes they are silent letters: **light daughter neighbour through**.

glue

Glue is sticky. You can stick things together with **glue**.

gnome

A **gnome** is a little person that you read about in stories. There is a model **gnome** in the garden.

goal

In football you try to kick the ball into the **goal**. Our team has scored two **goals**.

goat

A **goat** is an animal with horns. **Goats** give milk for people to drink.

gold

Gold is a shiny yellow metal. Things that are made of **gold** cost a lot of money.

goldfish

A **goldfish** is a small orange fish. Some people keep **goldfish** as pets.

good

Good is the opposite of bad. A **good** child in not naughty. A **good** book is nice to read. **Good** work is done well.

goodbye

We say **goodbye** when we are going away. We also say **goodbye** to somebody who is going away.

goose

A **goose** is a bird that looks like a big duck. You can see **geese** on a farm.

grass

Grass is a plant that covers the ground with thin green leaves. **Grass** grows in fields and gardens.

greedy

A **greedy** person wants a lot of things. My **greedy** sister has eaten all the cakes.

green

Green is the colour of grass. The green dress is on the right below.

greenhouse

A **greenhouse** is made of glass. You can grow plants in a **greenhouse** because it is warm inside.

grey

Grey is the colour you make when you mix black and white. Here is a **grey** elephant.

ground

We walk on the **ground**. James dug a hole in the **ground** to plant the tree.

a b c d e f **g** h i j k l m

group

A **group** is a number of people or things that are together. A **group** of children watched the puppet show.

grow

To **grow** is to get bigger.

guard

To **guard** is to look after something. Our dog **guards** the house when we are out.

guess

If you don't know the answer, you can **guess**. A **guess** is sometimes right and sometimes wrong.

guitar

A **guitar** is a musical instrument. You play a **guitar** by touching the strings.

gum

Your **gums** are the skin around the bottom of your teeth.

Gum is also a sweet that you can chew.

Another kind of **gum** is used to stick things together.

gun

A **gun** is used to shoot. The hunter was carrying a **gun**.

gymnastics

When you do **gymnastics**, you bend your body and turn upside down and do other exercises.

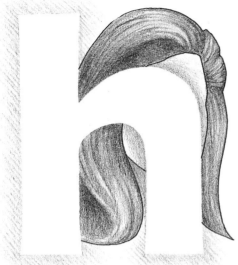

hand

Your **hand** is at the end of your arm. We have two **hands**.

handkerchief

A **handkerchief** is a small piece of cloth. You use a **handkerchief** to blow your nose or to wipe your eyes.

handle

We get hold of a **handle** to pick something up. Cups and pans have **handles**.

hang

To **hang** is to hold something at the top. **Hang** your coat on the peg. The wet washing is **hanging** on the clothes line.

happen

What **happened** at the party? What did you do there? Press the button and see what **happens**. Why do accidents always **happen** to me?

happy

Happy means pleased. You are **happy** when you are having fun. **Happy** is the opposite of sad.

harbour

A **harbour** is a stretch of water that is close to land. Ships stay in the **harbour** until they sail.

hard

Something that is **hard** takes a lot of time and effort. It is **hard** to swim with all your clothes on.
   Hard also means firm and not soft. Stones are **hard**.

harvest

Harvest is the time when fruit is picked and crops are cut because they are ripe.

hat

You wear a **hat** on your head. There are many different kinds of **hats**.

hate

If you **hate** something, you do not like it at all.

head

Your **head** is the part of your body that is above your neck. Your face is on the front of your **head**.

hear

We **hear** sounds with our ears. Did you **hear** the bell ring?

heart

Your **heart** is inside your chest. Your **heart** beats and keeps you alive.

heavy

Something that is **heavy** weighs a lot. It is hard to pick up a **heavy** case.

hair

Hair grows on your head. My sister has brown curly **hair**.

half

When you cut something into two equal pieces, each piece is a **half**. The pear has been cut in **half**. There are two **halves**.

hammer

You hit nails with a **hammer** to push them in.

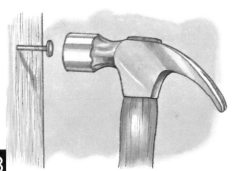

a b c d e f g **h** i j k l m

hedgehog

A **hedgehog** is an animal that has sharp spikes all over its body.

heel

Your **heel** is at the back of your foot. The **heel** of a shoe is the back part that we walk on.

helicopter

A **helicopter** is a machine that flies. The blades on the top of the **helicopter** turn round to lift it into the air.

hello

We say **hello** when we meet somebody.

helmet

A **helmet** is a hard hat. You wear a **helmet** so that your head will not get hurt.

help

To **help** is to do something for somebody. I **helped** my father wash the car.

hibernate

When an animal **hibernates**, it sleeps all through the winter.

hide

To **hide** is to put something in a place where nobody can see it. Let's **hide** behind the door.

high

Something that is **high** goes up a long way above the ground. Aeroplanes fly **high** in the sky. There is snow on the top of **high** mountains.

hill

A **hill** is a piece of ground that slopes up and down. The children have climbed to the top of the **hill**.

hit

To **hit** is to bring two things together with a bump. You can **hit** a ball with a bat. Mind you don't **hit** your head on the table.

hold

When you **hold** something, you keep it in your hand.

spelling tip

The letter **h** helps to make the sounds **ch, sh,** and **th**. Read these words:
chain watch shoe fish thin bath this clothes.
Did you notice that the sound **th** is different in the words **thin** and **this**?

When the letter **h** comes after the letter **p** it makes a sound like the letter **f**: **photograph telephone**.
The letter **h** is sometimes a silent letter. You do not say the letter **h** in these words: **honest ghost wheel rhyme**.

hole

A **hole** is an empty space. The men are digging a **hole** in the road.

holiday

A **holiday** is a day when there is no school and no work. We went to the seaside for our **holidays**.

hollow

Something that is **hollow** has an empty space inside it.

home

Your **home** is where you live. What time do you come **home** from school?

honest

An **honest** person tells the truth.

hook

A **hook** is a piece of metal that is bent or curved. You can hang things on a **hook**.

photograph

goldfish

cage

radio

drawer

cushion

fire

book

chair

crayons

At home

hop

To **hop** is to jump on one leg.

hope

When you **hope**, you want something to happen. I **hope** my father has bought me a present. I **hope** it won't rain tomorrow.

horse

A **horse** is a large animal. You can ride on a **horse**.

hose

A **hose** is a long pipe. Water goes through a **hose**. You can use a **hose** to water the garden or to wash a car.

hospital

A **hospital** is where doctors and nurses look after people who are ill.

hot

Hot is the opposite of cold. The sun is **hot**.

hotel

A **hotel** is a place where you can sleep and eat away from home.

hour

An **hour** is 60 minutes. There are 24 **hours** in a day. The show lasts for two **hours**, from three o'clock until five o'clock.

house

A **house** is a building where people live.

hungry

When you are **hungry**, you want to eat.

hurry

To **hurry** is to do something quickly. David **hurried** to school because he was late.

hurt

To **hurt** is to make something sore and painful. I fell over this morning and my leg **hurts**.

husband

A woman's **husband** is the man she is married to. My father is my mother's **husband**.

curtains

television

cupboard

ice

Ice is frozen water. **Ice** is cold and hard. In winter, in some countries, the rivers freeze and people skate on the **ice**.

ice cream

Ice cream is cold and sweet and nice to eat. I sometimes buy an **ice cream** on my way home from school.

idea

When you have an **idea**, you think of something. Let's use this piece of wood as a bat. That's a good **idea**!

igloo

An **igloo** is a house that is built from lumps of ice.

ill

To be **ill**, means to be sick or unwell. If you are **ill**, you see the doctor.

impossible

Something that is **impossible** cannot be done. It is **impossible** to count every grain of sand on the beach.

ink

Ink is a coloured liquid. There is **ink** in the pens that we write with.

insect

An **insect** is a small animal with six legs. Ants and bees and butterflies are **insects**.

inside

Inside is the opposite of outside. We keep things **inside** a box. There are rooms **inside** a house.

invisible

You cannot see something that is **invisible**. It is dangerous to drive in fog. Cars become **invisible**.

invite

To **invite** is to ask somebody to come. I have **invited** all my friends to my birthday party.

iron

We use an **iron** to press the creases out of our clothes.

Iron is also a kind of metal.

island

An **island** is a piece of land that is surrounded by water. There is an **island** in the middle of the lake. Great Britain is an **island**.

jacket

A **jacket** is a short coat. Emma is wearing a red **jacket**.

jam

Jam is sweet and nice to eat. You can spread **jam** on bread. **Jam** is made from fruit and sugar.

January

January is the first month of the year. **January** comes before February.

jar

A **jar** is a glass pot. Jam and honey are kept in **jars**.

jeans

Jeans are trousers that are made of strong material.

jelly

Jelly is a sweet food. When you make a **jelly**, you have to wait until it is cool and firm before you can eat it.

jigsaw

A **jigsaw** is a kind of puzzle. You have to fit all the pieces of the **jigsaw** together to make a picture.

join

To **join** is to put things together. I **joined** the two ropes together with a knot. When you **join** a club, you become a member.

joke

A **joke** makes people laugh. My brother told me a **joke** about an elephant.

n o p q r s t u v w x y z

jug

A **jug** is used to hold milk or water and to pour it out. The boy in the picture is carrying a jug of milk to the tea-table.

juice

Juice is the liquid that comes out of fruit when you squeeze it. May I have a drink of orange **juice**, please?

July

July is the seventh month of the year. **July** comes after June and before August.

jump

When you **jump**, you go up in the air with both feet off the ground. The dog **jumped** over the fence.

At teatime

44

a b c d e f g h i **j** k l m

jumper

A **jumper** is a piece of warm clothing that you wear on the top half of your body. My mother knitted a pink **jumper** for my sister.

June

June is the sixth month of the year. **June** comes after May and before July.

jungle

A **jungle** is a forest in a hot country. Monkeys live in the **jungle**. The trees and plants grow very close together in a **jungle**.

jug

son

jigsaw

kangaroo

A **kangaroo** is an animal with strong back legs for

jumping. **Kangaroos** live in Australia. The mother carries her baby in a pouch.

oven

bag

knee

kittens

mug

knife

biscuit

In the kitchen

a b c d e f g h i j **k** l m

keep

If you **keep** something, you do not give it away. You can **keep** this book, I don't want it back.

To **keep** is also to put something somewhere. I **keep** my socks in this drawer.

kettle

You boil water in a **kettle**. Some **kettles** are heated by electricity, others are heated on the cooker.

key

A **key** is used to open or close a lock. You lock a

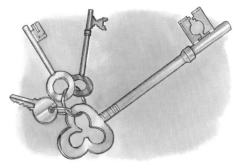

door with a **key**. You also need a **key** to start a car.

kick

To **kick** is to hit something with your foot. Robert **kicked** the ball into the goal.

kill

To **kill** is to make something or somebody die. The cold weather will **kill** our plants. Many people were **killed** in the war.

kind

Kind means nice and gentle. A **kind** person helps other people. It was very **kind** of you to do all the washing up.

Kind also means sort or type. Oranges and bananas are different **kinds** of fruit.

king

A **king** is a man who rules a country. A **king** lives in a palace.

kiss

When you **kiss**, you touch a person's cheek or mouth with your lips. My mother always gives me a **kiss** before I go to bed.

kitchen

The **kitchen** is the room where food is cooked.

kite

A **kite** flies high in the air at the end of a long string.

kitten

A **kitten** is a young cat.

knee

Your **knee** is the place where your leg bends.

kneel

When you **kneel**, you bend your legs and put your **knees** on the ground. The girl in the kitchen is **kneeling** beside the kittens.

knife

A **knife** is used for cutting things. **Knives** are sharp.

knit

You **knit** with wool and **knitting** needles. Sarah is **knitting** a scarf.

knock

To **knock** is to hit something. Who **knocked** the chair over? When you **knock** at the door, you make a noise by hitting it.

knot

We tie a **knot** to hold something tightly or to join two ends together. It is sometimes hard to undo a **knot**.

know

You **know** something that is in your mind. I **know** how to speak French.

spelling tip

The letter **k** is sometimes a silent letter. You do not say the letter **k** in these words: **knee knife knit knot know**. Some other words have silent letters: You do not say the letter **b** in these words: **comb lamb**. You do not say the letter **g** in these words: **gnome sign**. You do not say the letter **h** in these words: **honest ghost**.

a b c d e f g h i j **k** l m

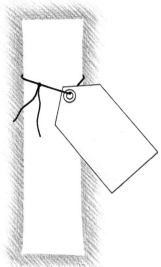

label

You put a **label** on something to tell people about it. The **label** on a tin of food tells us what is inside.

ladder

A **ladder** is a set of steps that is used to reach high places. My brother climbed up a **ladder** to reach the top of the slide.

lake

A **lake** is water that is surrounded by land.

lamb

A **lamb** is a young sheep.

land

The **land** is the solid part of the earth that is not covered with water.

When something **lands**, it comes down to the ground. The aeroplane **landed** in a field.

language

Language is all the words that we say or write. Different countries have different **languages**.

large

Large means big. Joanne has a **large** present, her brother has a small one.

last

Last means at the end. If you eat the **last** biscuit, there will be no more left.

late

Late is the opposite of early. We were **late** for the show, it had already started when we arrived.

laugh

People **laugh** when they see or hear something funny. The teacher told a joke and all the children **laughed**.

law

A **law** is a rule that everybody in the country has to obey. The thief was sent to prison for breaking the **law**.

lay

To **lay** is to put something down carefully. **Lay** the baby in his cot.

lazy

A **lazy** person never wants to do any work. My **lazy** sister stayed in bed all morning.

lead

To **lead** is to show somebody the way. We asked Peter to **lead** us to the park. Peter went ahead and we followed.

leaf

A **leaf** is the flat green part of a plant. In summer

the trees are covered with **leaves**.

At the zoo

a b c d e f g h i j k **l** m

lean

When something **leans**, it is sloping. If you **lean** on something, you press on it or rest against it.

learn

To **learn** is to find out. You go to school to learn. I am **learning** how to play the piano.

leave

To **leave** is to go away. My father **leaves** work at six o'clock.

left

Left is the opposite of right. When you read or write, you start at the **left** side of the page.

leg

Your **leg** is the part of your body that you walk with. People have two **legs**, dogs have four **legs**, and ants have six **legs**.

lemon

A **lemon** is a fruit with a yellow skin. **Lemons** have a sour taste.

lend

Will you **lend** me your scissors? I'll give them back to you when I've finished cutting out my picture.

leopard

A **leopard** is a wild animal with spots all over its fur. You can see **leopards** at the zoo.

less

Less means not as much. I have **less** money than my sister. She has five pounds but I only have three pounds.

lesson

You learn something in a **lesson**. We had a French **lesson** at school today.

let

To **let** is to say that somebody may do something. Will you **let** me ride your bicycle?

camel

cage

monkey

brush

leg

elephant

n o p q r s t u v w x y z

letter

You write a **letter** to tell somebody something. Thomas wrote a **letter** to his aunt to thank her for the birthday present she sent him.

A **letter** is also part of a word. There are 26 different **letters**: a, b, c, d, e, f, ...

library

A **library** is a place where books are kept. You can usually borrow books from a **library**.

lick

To **lick** is to pass your tongue over something. You **lick** food to taste it or to eat it. I **licked** the jam off my fingers.

lid

A **lid** is a cover for a box or a tin. Pans and jars also have **lids**.

lie

To **lie** is to rest flat. At night you **lie** down on your bed and go to sleep.

When you tell a **lie**, you say something that is not true. Honest people never **lie**.

life

Life is being alive. Your **life** begins when you are born and ends when you die.

lift

To **lift** is to pick something up. I can't **lift** this heavy case.

light

Light helps us to see. It comes from the sun or from an electric **light**. **Light** is the opposite of dark.

Light also means not heavy. A feather is **light**, it does not weigh very much.

lightning

Lightning is a flash of light in the sky during a storm. **Lightning** comes before thunder.

like

If you **like** something, you think it is nice. I **like** playing with my toys. Do you **like** chocolate?

Like also means nearly the same. Claire's dress is **like** her sister's.

line

A **line** is a long thin mark. Can you draw a straight **line** without using a ruler?

lion

A **lion** is a wild animal. You can see **lions** at the zoo.

lip

Your **lips** are the soft parts at the edge of your mouth.

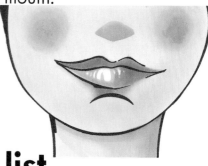

list

When we make a **list**, we write down the names of people or things that we want to remember. A shopping **list** tells you all the things you want to buy.

a b c d e f g h i j k **l** m

listen

To **listen** is to take notice of something that you hear. I **listen** to the radio in the morning.

litter

Litter is paper and cans and other things that people have thrown away. You should never drop **litter** on the ground.

little

Little is the opposite of big. A mouse is a **little** animal.

live

To **live** is to be alive. I **live** with my parents in Park Road. Our home is in Park Road.

LETTERS

Do you know what an ENTHAPEL is? The letters are all mixed up. If you put the letters in a different order you can make the word ELEPHANT.

Here are some more mixed-up animals. Can you put the letters in the right order?

USMOE
PORELAD
ERBAZ
BIRTAB
AGORKONA

Here are some mixed-up vegetables and fruit:

TAPOOT
ROTRAC
NINOO
PALEP
ANABAN

Here are some longer mixed-up words. There are some clues to help you.

TRAPMURSEEK (a shop)
HOGPATHORP (a kind of picture)
BREMPESTE (a month)
RAPPEWENS (something to read)
DARTASYU (a day)

Answers on page 96

lock

We **lock** a door by turning the key in the lock. When the door is **locked** nobody can open it.

long

Long means large from end to end. A giraffe has a **long** neck.

look

To **look** is to take notice of something that you see. I **looked** at the pictures in the book.

loose

Loose means not fixed or not tight. One of my teeth is **loose**, I can move it around.

lose

If you **lose** something, you do not have it any more. You won't be able to open the door if you **lose** your key.

loud

Loud means noisy. The music was so loud, we could hear it in the next room.

love

To **love** is to like very much. I **love** my baby sister.

low

Low is the opposite of high. It is easy to climb over a **low** wall. A **low** shelf is near the floor.

lunch

Lunch is the meal that we eat in the middle of the day.

n o p q r s t u v w x y z

machine

A **machine** is something that does work for us. A washing **machine** washes our clothes.

magazine

A **magazine** is like a large thin book. My father

helicopter

advertisement

hotel

bus

van

bicycle

man

machine

helmet

pavement

hole

How many machines can you see in the street?

a b c d e f g h i j k l **m**

buys a **magazine** about cars every week.

magic

Magic makes impossible things seem to happen. My uncle made the handkerchief disappear by **magic**.

magnet

A **magnet** is made of metal. Pins and nails and other metal things stick to a **magnet**.

make

You **make** something by putting things together. I am **making** a model aeroplane.

man

A **man** is a male adult. Your father and your uncle are **men**.

many

Many means a lot. **Many** children like sweets.

map

A **map** shows us where places are. A **map** of a town has all the roads on it. A **map** of the world has all the countries on it.

March

March is the third month of the year. **March** comes after February and before April.

mark

A **mark** is a spot or a patch. There is a dirty **mark** on your shirt.

market

You can buy lots of different things at a **market**. **Markets** are usually outside.

marry

A man and a woman **marry** each other at a wedding. People get **married** because they love each other.

mask

You wear a **mask** over your face to make yourself look different.

hospital

coach

road

mat

A **mat** is used to cover a small part of the floor. Wipe your feet on the **mat** before you come in.

match

A **match** is a small stick that is used to make a flame.

A **match** is also a game of football or tennis or another sport.

To **match** is to go together. These two shoes don't **match**, one is brown and the other is blue.

May

May is the fifth month of the year. **May** comes after April and before June.

meal

Breakfast and dinner are **meals**. People usually sit at a table to eat their **meals**.

mean

Large **means** big. It is the same thing.

A **mean** person is not kind. My sister is **mean**, she never lets me play with her toys.

measure

When you **measure** something, you find out how big it is.

meat

Meat is the part of an animal that we eat as food. Beef and lamb and pork are kinds of **meat**.

medicine

You take **medicine** to help you get better when you are ill. My mother bought a bottle of cough **medicine** at the chemist's shop.

meet

When people **meet**, they come to the same place. I often **meet** my friends at the bus stop.

melt

Hard or cold things **melt** when they become warm. When ice **melts**, it changes back into water.

mend

You **mend** something that is broken or torn. My father **mended** the broken vase with glue. He stuck the pieces back together.

metal

Metal is hard and strong. Pins, knives, pans and cars are made of **metal**.

middle

The **middle** of something is the same distance from all its sides. There is a tree in the **middle** of the garden.

milk

Milk is a white drink that comes from cows.

minute

A **minute** is 60 seconds. There are 60 **minutes** in an hour. I waited for ten **minutes**, from three o'clock until ten past three.

mirror

When you look in a **mirror**, you can see yourself. **Mirrors** are made of glass.

miss

If you **miss** something, you do not catch it or hit it. James had to walk to school because he **missed** the bus.

To **miss** also means to be sad because somebody is not with you. I **missed** my brother when he went to camp.

mistake

A **mistake** is something you have done that is wrong.

mix

To **mix** is to put things together. You **mix** black paint with white paint to make grey.

Monday

Monday is one of the days of the week. **Monday** comes after Sunday and before Tuesday.

money

Money is the coins and notes that you use to buy things.

monkey

A **monkey** is an animal. **Monkeys** live in the trees in hot countries.

monster

A **monster** is a horrible creature that you read about in stories.

month

There are twelve **months** in a year. The first **month** is January. Do you know the names of the other **months**?

moon

The **moon** shines in the sky at night.

more

More means a larger amount. I have **more** cars than my brother. He has six cars but I have ten.

morning

The **morning** is the first part of the day. You get out of bed in the **morning**.

mother

Your **mother** is the woman in your family. Mrs Brown has a child called Steven. Mrs Brown is Steven's **mother**.

mountain

A **mountain** is a piece of land that goes up very high. The highest **mountain** in the world is Mount Everest.

mouse

A **mouse** is a small animal with a long tail. **Mice** live in fields and houses.

moustache

A **moustache** is the hair that grows above a man's mouth.

mouth

Your **mouth** is part of your face. You use your **mouth** to eat and to talk.

move

To **move** is to go to a different place. I **moved** the chair closer to the window.

mud

Mud is soft wet earth. My father's boots were covered with **mud** when he came in from the garden.

mug

A **mug** is a large cup.

muscle

Our **muscles** are inside our bodies. **Muscles** help you to move parts of your body.

music

Music is the nice sounds made by musical instruments or singing voices. The teacher played some **music** on the piano.

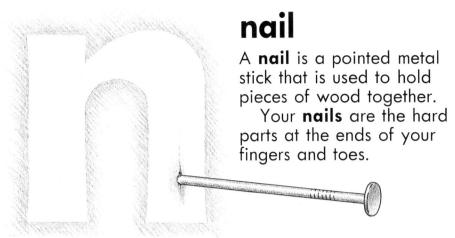

nail

A **nail** is a pointed metal stick that is used to hold pieces of wood together.

Your **nails** are the hard parts at the ends of your fingers and toes.

name

Your **name** is what you are called. My **name** is Lucy.

narrow

Narrow means small from side to side. The road is very **narrow**, there is not enough room for two cars to pass each other.

shop

newspapers

brother

sister

comic

neck

Buying a newspaper

a b c d e f g h i j k l m

naughty

If you are **naughty**, you do things that you should not do. A **naughty** child is not good.

near

Near means not far. My friend's house is **near** the station. She can see the trains from her bedroom window.

nearly

Nearly tells us that something will happen soon. I have **nearly** finished reading my book. I only have one page left to read.

neat

Something that is **neat** looks nice and tidy. David's desk is very **neat**.

neck

Your **neck** is the part of your body between your head and your shoulders.

need

If you **need** something, you must have it. I **need** some money to buy my newspaper.

needle

A **needle** is a thin piece of metal with a point at one end and a little hole at the other. **Needles** are used for sewing.

neighbour

Your **neighbour** is a person who lives near you.

nest

Birds lay their eggs in **nests**. A bird's **nest** is made of sticks and leaves.

bird

bank

nurse

shoe

notice

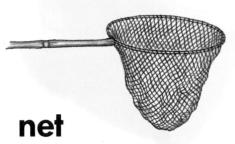

net

You can use a **net** to catch fish. The water runs out through the holes in the **net**.

never

Never means not at any time. I have **never** been to Africa.

new

Something that is **new** has just been made. My father bought a **new** pair of shoes because his old ones were worn out.

news

News tells us about things that have just happened. We listened to the **news** on the radio.

newspaper

Newspapers are printed every day to tell people the news. I read about the space mission in the **newspaper**.

next

Next means the one that comes after. If we miss this train, we'll have to wait for the **next** one.

night

The **night** is the time when it is dark outside. People sleep during the **night**.

nine

Nine is the number that comes after eight. Here are **nine** buttons.

noise

A **noise** is a loud sound. The children were making a lot of **noise**.

nose

Your **nose** is in the middle of your face. You use your **nose** to breathe and to smell.

note

A **note** is a short letter. A **note** is also a piece of paper that is used as money.

nothing

Nothing means not anything. There is **nothing** in this glass. It is empty.

notice

A **notice** is a sign that tells us something. The teacher put up a **notice** with the date of the football match on it.

November

November is the eleventh month of the year. **November** comes after October and before December.

now

Now means at this time. I don't want a drink **now**, I'll have one later.

number

A **number** tells us how many. 6, 13, 487, and 2,905 are all **numbers**.

nurse

A **nurse** looks after people in hospital.

nut

A **nut** has a hard shell. The inside of some **nuts** is nice to eat. **Nuts** grow on trees and bushes.

a b c d e f g h i j k l m

old

Old means not new. My **old** coat doesn't fit me any more. **Old** people have been alive for a long time.

one

One is the first number. There is only **one** horse in the field.

onion

An **onion** is a vegetable that grows under the ground. **Onions** have a very strong taste.

only

I invited eight people to my party, but **only** three of them came. **Only** one of the apples is red, the others are green.

obey

To **obey** is to do what somebody tells you to do.

October

October is the tenth month of the year. **October** comes after September and before November.

octopus

An **octopus** is an animal that lives in the sea. An **octopus** has eight long arms.

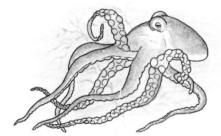

office

An **office** is a room where adults sit at desks and work.

oil

Oil is used to make machines run smoothly. A different kind of **oil** is used for frying food.

n o p q r s t u v w x y z

OPPOSITES

The opposite of **hot** is **cold**. Hot means not cold. Can you match these words with their opposites?

rough	light	low	large	rich	quick
old	slow	poor	fat	new	hard
open	quiet	thin	smooth	narrow	loud
small	wide	soft	high	shut	heavy

Answers on page 96

open

Open means not shut. When you **open** a box, you take the lid off. The door was **open**, so I went in.

opposite

Hot is the **opposite** of cold. Hot means not cold.

Opposite also means on the other side. Julie is sitting **opposite** her brother.

orange

An **orange** is a round fruit with a thick skin. You can peel the skin off the **orange** and eat the fruit inside.

Orange is also the colour of an **orange**.

order

Order is the way things are arranged. We lined up in **order** of size, with the smallest person at the front and the tallest at the back.

ordinary

Ordinary means usual and not different. You can't write on the label with an **ordinary** pen, you need a pen with special ink in it.

other

The **other** one is not this one. My chair was broken, so I sat on one of the **other** chairs.

outside

Outside means not in a building. You can't play **outside** if it's raining. The **outside** of something is the part that you can see.

oven

We can bake cakes and roast meat in an **oven**.

over

Over means higher. The birds flew **over** the house.

owl

An **owl** is a bird that flies at night.

own

To **own** is to have something. I **own** this bicycle, it is mine. This is my **own** bicycle, it belongs to me.

On your **own** means by yourself. If you go to school on your **own**, nobody goes with you.

a b c d e f g h i j k l m

p

pack

To **pack** is to put something inside another. I **packed** all my clothes into the bag.

page

A **page** is a piece of paper in a book. Most of the **pages** in this book have writing and pictures on them.

pain

A **pain** is what you feel when part of your body is hurt.

paint

Paint is coloured liquid that is used to make pictures and to cover doors and walls. My father **painted** the chairs red to match the new table.

pair

A **pair** is two things that are used together. I bought a **pair** of white socks.

palace

A **palace** is a large building where a king or queen lives.

pan

A **pan** is used to cook food on a cooker. Most **pans** are made of metal.

paper

Paper is thin and flat. We write and draw on **paper**. The pages of a book are made of **paper**.

parachute

A **parachute** is a large round piece of cloth shaped like an umbrella. A **parachute** helps a person to fall slowly through the air.

parent

Your **parents** are your mother and your father.

park

A **park** is a place where anybody can go to walk or play. **Parks** usually have grass and flowers and swings and slides.

part

A **part** of something is not all of it. Your leg is **part** of your body. I have only cleaned **part** of the floor, the rest of it is still dirty.

party

You have fun with your friends at a **party**. My sister is having a birthday **party** tomorrow.

pass

To **pass** is to go by. I **pass** the supermarket on my way to school.

past

The **past** is the time that has already gone. Yesterday and last week are in the **past**.

path

A **path** is a strip of ground that you can walk on. We cleared a **path** through the snow. There is a **path** along the edge of the river.

pattern

A **pattern** is the way shapes and colours are arranged. There is a **pattern** of red and black stars on the wallpaper.

pavement

The **pavement** is a path by the side of a road. People walk on the **pavement**.

63

n o p q r s t u v w x y z

paw

A **paw** is an animal's foot.

pay

To **pay** is to give somebody money for something. You have to **pay** to go on the roundabout.

pear

A **pear** is a fruit that you can eat. **Pears** grow on trees.

pedal

You push a **pedal** with your foot to make something move. Bicycles have **pedals**.

peel

To **peel** is to take the skin off a fruit or a vegetable.

pictures

timetable

page

badge

paint

paper

At school

a b c d e f g h i j k l m

pen

You can write with a **pen**. **Pens** have ink inside them.

pencil

We use a **pencil** for writing or for drawing.

penguin

A **penguin** is a black and white bird that lives in cold places. **Penguins** can swim but they cannot fly.

people

Girls, boys, men and women are all **people**.

person

A **person** is a girl or a boy or a man or a woman.

pet

A **pet** is an animal that we keep at home. Do you have any **pets**?

petrol

Petrol is the liquid that makes cars go. The car stopped because it had run out of **petrol**.

photograph

When you take a **photograph**, you use a camera to make a picture of what you see. A **photograph** is sometimes called a photo.

pick

To **pick** is to decide what you want. The teacher **picked** four children to help him.

picnic

A **picnic** is a meal that you eat outside. We had a **picnic** in the park.

picture

A **picture** is a drawing, a painting, or a photograph. There are lots of **pictures** on the wall.

plants

teacher

tie

pocket

pen

pencil

ruler

rubber

pie

A **pie** is a kind of food. A **pie** is made of pastry with fruit or meat inside.

piece

A **piece** is part of something. Cut the cake into six **pieces**.

pig

A **pig** is an animal with a curly tail. You can see **pigs** on a farm.

pile

A **pile** is a lot of things on top of each other.

pillow

A **pillow** is a soft pad on a bed. You put your head on the **pillow**.

pin

A **pin** is a thin piece of metal with a point at one

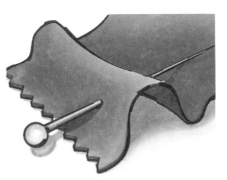

end. A **pin** is used to hold things together.

pink

Pink is the colour you make when you mix red and white. Here is a **pink** flower.

plant

A **plant** is a living thing. **Plants** have leaves and roots.

To **plant** is to put something in soil so that it can grow. I **planted** a tree in the garden.

plastic

Many things are made of **plastic**. **Plastic** cups and plates do not break if you drop them.

plate

A **plate** is flat and round. We eat food from a **plate**.

platform

A **platform** is higher than the floor of a room. The headmistress stood on the **platform** to make a speech.

play

To **play** is to have fun. I like **playing** with my friends.

please

We say **please** when we are asking for something. May I have a drink of water, **please?**

pocket

You can put things in a **pocket**. Coats and trousers and other clothes have **pockets**. The teacher has a handkerchief in his **pocket**.

point

A **point** is sharp. Pins and pencils and nails and needles have **points**.

When you **point**, you use your finger to show something. **Point** to the book you want.

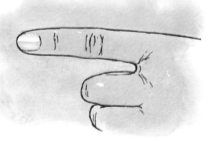

poison

Poison is used to kill rats and mice and other animals. You will be very ill if you eat **poison**.

police

The **police** make sure that people obey the law.

polish

To **polish** is to make something shine. I **polished** my silver necklace.

poor

A **poor** person does not have much money. **Poor** is the opposite of rich.

post

When you send a letter by **post**, you put a stamp on it and put it in a special box. You can **post** a letter to anywhere in the world.

potato

A **potato** is a vegetable that grows under the ground. Chips and crisps are made from **potatoes**.

pour

When we **pour** liquid, it goes from one thing into another. I **poured** some milk from the jug into my cup.

powder

Powder is a lot of very tiny bits. Flour and sand are kinds of **powder**.

pram

A **pram** is a baby's bed with wheels and a handle.

PAST

When we talk or write about doing something in the past, we usually use a word that ends with **ed**:

play	I **played** with my friends yesterday.
bake	My mother **baked** a cake last week.

Sometimes we have to use a different word:

buy	Jennifer **bought** a comic.
catch	Steven **caught** the ball.
do	My sister **did** her homework.
eat	The dog **ate** his dinner.
fight	My grandfather **fought** in the war.
go	The children **went** to school.
have	Paul **had** four sweets.
know	Sarah **knew** the answer.
leave	The train **left** the station.
make	My brother **made** a mistake.
run	The cat **ran** away.
sit	Jonathan **sat** down.
take	Claire **took** her new pen to school.
wear	I **wore** my blue coat.

You can push a **pram** along the pavement.

present

A **present** is something that you give to somebody. This watch was a birthday **present** from my grandmother.

press

To **press** is to push hard on something. You have to **press** this button to make the machine work.

pretend

If you **pretend** to do something, you do not really do it. I **pretended** to be an astronaut walking on the moon.

pretty

A **pretty** person or thing is nice to look at. What a **pretty** dress!

price

The **price** of something tells you how much money you need to buy it.

prince

A **prince** is the son of a king or queen.

princess

A **princess** is the daughter of a king or queen.

print

To **print** is to make a mark by pressing on something. You can **print** patterns on a piece of paper or cloth. Words are **printed** on the pages of books.

prison

Prison is a place for people who have done something wrong. The doors of the **prison** are locked so that nobody can escape.

prize

A **prize** is something that you win. My brother won first **prize** in the painting competition.

programme

A **programme** is a show on television or radio. We watched an interesting television **programme** about butterflies.

promise

If you **promise** to do something, you must do it. I can't go to the park after school, I **promised** my mother that I would come straight home.

proud

I am **proud** of this picture. I painted it myself and I think it is very good. If I win the competition, my parents will be **proud** of me.

puddle

A **puddle** is a small patch of water on the ground. It rained all day and there were lots of **puddles** in the road.

pull

When you **pull** something, it moves towards you. You can also **pull** something along behind you.

puppet

A **puppet** is a doll with strings on parts of its body. When you pull the strings, the **puppet** moves. A different kind of **puppet** moves when you put your hand inside it, like a glove.

puppy

A **puppy** is a young dog.

purple

Purple is the colour you make when you mix red and blue. Here is a **purple** jelly.

purse

A **purse** is a small bag. You can keep money in a **purse**.

push

When you **push** something, it moves away from you. You can also **push** something along in front of you.

put

To **put** is to move something somewhere and leave it there. **Put** the plates on the table.

puzzle

It is hard to find the answer to a **puzzle**. **Puzzles** make you think. A jigsaw is a kind of **puzzle**.

pyjamas

People wear **pyjamas** in bed. **Pyjamas** cover all your body to keep you warm.

quarter

When you cut something into four equal pieces, each piece is a **quarter**.

queen

A **queen** is a woman who rules a country. The wife of a king is also a **queen**.

question

You ask a **question** when you want an answer. 'What is your name?' is a **question**.

queue

A **queue** is a line of people who are waiting for something.

quick

If you are **quick**, you do something in a very short time. Be **quick**! The train is about to go!

quiet

To be **quiet** is to make no sound or not much noise. Be **quiet**, the baby is asleep.

quilt

A **quilt** is a warm thick cover for a bed.

quiz

A **quiz** is a number of questions. A **quiz** can be a test or a competition or a game.

QUIZ

Here are twenty questions. You can find all the answers in this dictionary.

1 What do you keep in a **garage**?
2 What colour is a **tomato**?
3 How many legs does a **spider** have?
4 Which month comes after **October**?
5 What is an **igloo** made of?
6 Where does a **king** live?
7 How do you make the colour **purple**?
8 What comes after **lightning**?
9 What do we use a **camera** for?
10 Where does **milk** come from?
11 What is the opposite of **empty**?
12 What can you buy in a **restaurant**?
13 When do we eat **breakfast**?
14 How do you play a **drum**?
15 Which day comes before **Friday**?
16 Where is your **nose**?
17 Why do you wear an **apron**?
18 What does a **thermometer** tell us?
19 When do you need an **umbrella**?
20 How many wheels does a **bicycle** have?

Answers on page 96

n o p **q** r s t u v w x y z

rabbit

A **rabbit** is a small animal with long ears and a short tail. **Rabbits** live in holes in the ground.

race

In a **race**, the person who goes fastest is the winner.

radio

A **radio** is a machine that we listen to. You can hear music and other programmes on the **radio**.

railway

Trains run on a **railway**.

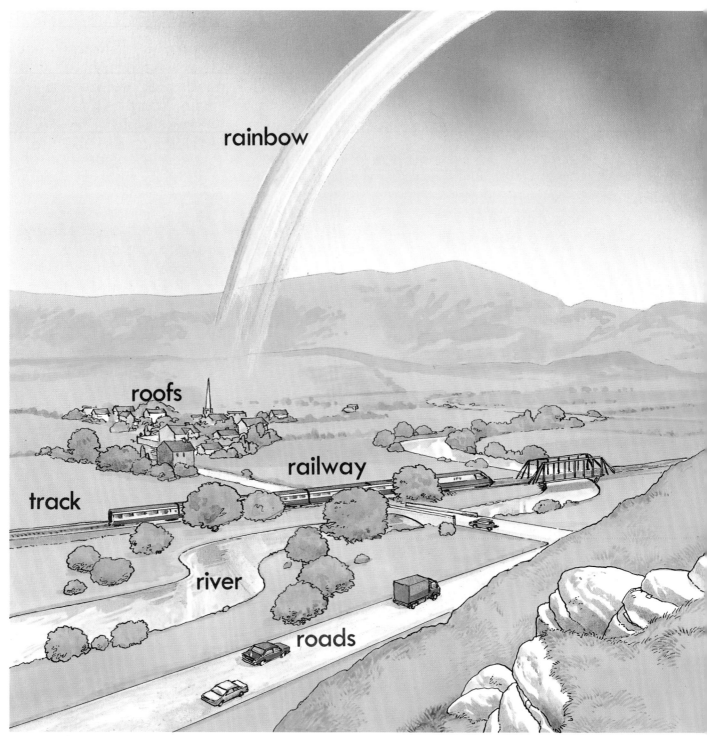

rainbow

roofs

railway

track

river

roads

The rainbow

a b c d e f g h i j k l m

rain

Rain is water that falls from clouds in the sky. It is **raining** today.

rainbow

You sometimes see a **rainbow** in the sky when there is rain and sun at the same time. A **rainbow** is a curved band of colours.

rattle

A **rattle** makes a tapping noise when you shake it. The marbles **rattled** inside the box.

reach

To **reach** is to get to. The shelf is too high, I can't **reach** it.

read

To **read** is to look at words and understand them. I like **reading** adventure stories.

ready

When you are **ready**, you have done everything you need to do before you begin. I'm **ready** for bed. I've had a bath, I've put my pyjamas on, and I've cleaned my teeth.

real

A doll is not a **real** baby. Dragons are not **real**, they are just things that you read about in stories.

record

A **record** is a round piece of plastic with a hole in the middle. When you play a **record** you hear music or other sounds.

red

Red is the colour of a ripe tomato. Here is a **red** hat.

clouds

wife

husband

radio

rabbit

refrigerator

A **refrigerator** is a cupboard that is cold inside. We keep food and drinks cool and fresh in a **refrigerator** in the kitchen. A **refrigerator** is sometimes called a fridge.

remember

When you **remember** something, it stays in your mind. Can you **remember** what you had for dinner yesterday?

rescue

To **rescue** is to save somebody from something bad. The fireman **rescued** the children from the burning house.

rest

When you **rest**, you sit down or lie down because you are tired. I've been working all morning, I need a **rest**.

The **rest** means the others. Three children stayed in to help the teacher and the **rest** of the class went out to play.

restaurant

A **restaurant** is a place where you can buy and eat a meal.

rhyme

To **rhyme** is to end with the same sound. The word 'plate' **rhymes** with the word 'wait'.

ribbon

A **ribbon** is a long strip of coloured cloth. Some girls tie **ribbons** in their hair.

rice

Rice is a kind of food. **Rice** is small hard grains that become soft and white when they are cooked.

rich

A **rich** person has a lot of money. **Rich** is the opposite of poor.

ride

To **ride** is to travel on something that moves. You can **ride** a horse or a bicycle.

right

Right is the opposite of left. Andrew is holding up his **right** hand.

Right is also the opposite of wrong. The teacher has written the **right** answer on the board.

ring

A **ring** is a circle. A **ring** is also a piece of jewellery that you wear on your finger.

To **ring** is to make the sound of a bell. The telephone is **ringing**. **Ring** the bell and somebody will open the door.

ripe

When fruit is **ripe** it is ready to eat.

river

A **river** is a strip of water with land on both sides. **Rivers** go from the hills to the sea. We crossed the **river** in a boat.

road

A **road** is a strip of ground for cars to drive on. You go along a **road** to get from one place to another.

RHYME

When words rhyme, they have the same sound at the end. The word **seat** rhymes with **meet**. The word **play** rhymes with **say**. The word **cough** rhymes with **off**. Can you match these words with their rhymes?

write	red	hole	dead	comb	ache
bake	late	socks	lie	box	money
home	fry	dress	roll	fight	brick
car	thick	funny	less	eight	far

Answers on page 96

roast

You **roast** meat or potatoes in an oven. We had **roast** chicken for dinner.

rob

To **rob** is to steal something from a person or a place. I've been **robbed**! Somebody has stolen all my money!

rock

A **rock** is a large piece of stone. **Rock** is hard.

To **rock** is to move from side to side.

roll

To **roll** is to turn over and over. The ball **rolled** down the hill.

roof

A **roof** covers the top of a building.

room

A **room** is part of a building. The **room** where we sleep is called a bedroom. The **room** where we cook is called a kitchen.

root

The **root** of a plant is the part that grows under the ground.

rope

Rope is very thick string. **Rope** is used to tie up strong or heavy things.

rough

Rough is the opposite of smooth. A **rough** suface has a lot of lumps in it.

round

A ball is **round**. So is a circle.

row

A **row** is a line of things or people, side by side.

rub

To **rub** is to move something backwards and forwards on something else. I **rubbed** the dirty mark with a cloth.

rubber

You use a **rubber** to make pencil marks disappear.

Wellington boots and car tyres are made of **rubber**. A **rubber** band stretches. A **rubber** ball bounces.

rule

A **rule** tells you what you must do. Games have **rules**. You must obey the school **rules**.

To **rule** is to be in charge of a country. Kings and queens **rule**.

ruler

A **ruler** is a strip of wood or plastic. You can use a **ruler** to draw a straight line or to measure something.

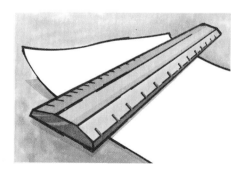

run

To **run** is to move along quickly using your legs.

runway

A **runway** is a strip of ground at an airport. Aeroplanes take off and land on a **runway**.

n o p q **r** s t u v w x y z

sad

Sad means not happy. Michael was very **sad** when his pet rabbit died.

safe

Safe means not dangerous. My father mended the broken chair to make it **safe** to sit on.

sail

A **sail** is a large piece of cloth. Some boats have **sails**. The wind blows on the **sail** and moves the boat along.

To **sail** is to travel in a boat.

same

Bananas and lemons are the **same** colour. Bananas are yellow and lemons are also yellow. **Same** is the opposite of different.

sand

Sand is the powder that covers the beach. Each grain of **sand** is a very tiny piece of rock.

sandal

A **sandal** is a shoe that we wear in the summer. **Sandals** help to keep your feet cool because they do not cover the whole of your feet.

sandwich

A **sandwich** is two pieces of bread with cheese or jam or other food between them.

Saturday

Saturday is one of the days of the week. **Saturday** comes after Friday and before Sunday.

sausage

A **sausage** is a kind of food. **Sausages** are made of tiny pieces of meat inside a thin skin tube.

save

To **save** is to keep. If you **save** money, you do not spend it.

When you **save** a person, you stop something bad from happening. All the people were **saved** from the sinking ship.

saw

A **saw** is a sharp tool that is used to cut wood.

say

When you speak you **say** something. I always **say** 'Thank you' when somebody gives me a present.

scarf

You wear a **scarf** around your neck to keep you warm. You can wear a different kind of **scarf** on your head.

school

We go to **school** to learn things. Do you like going to **school**?

scissors

Scissors are used to cut things. A pair of **scissors** has two sharp blades at one end and two holes for your fingers at the other. They are joined together in the middle.

scratch

To **scratch** something is to rub something sharp against it. The cat **scratched** the table with its claws. My leg was itchy, so I **scratched** it.

sea

The **sea** is the salt water that covers parts of the earth. We swim in the **sea** at the seaside. You can travel across the **sea** to another country.

season

There are four **seasons** in the year: spring, summer, autumn and winter.

a b c d e f g h i j k l m

seat

A **seat** is something to sit on. Chairs and stools are **seats**. Buses and trains have **seats**.

second

A **second** is a very short time. There are 60 **seconds** in a minute.
   Second also means the one after the first. Christopher won the race and I came **second**.

secret

A **secret** is something that you do not want anybody else to know. Can you keep a **secret**?

see

We **see** things with our eyes. Did you **see** that flash of lightning?

seed

A **seed** is part of a plant. New plants grow from **seeds**.

seesaw

A **seesaw** is a long piece of wood or metal with a seat at each end. You can play on a **seesaw** with your friend. When you go down, your friend goes up, and when your friend goes down, you go up.

sell

The baker **sells** bread. We give the baker some money and he gives us some bread.

send

To **send** is to make something go from one place to another. I'll **send** you a postcard when I get to Australia.

September

September is the ninth month of the year. **September** comes after August and before October.

seven

Seven is the number that comes after six. Here are **seven** sheep.

sew

When you **sew**, you use a needle and thread to join pieces of cloth together.

shadow

A **shadow** is the dark shape that you see when something is in front of the light. On a sunny day you can see your **shadow** on the ground.

shake

To **shake** is to move quickly up and down or from side to side. You have to **shake** the bottle to mix the cream with the milk.

shape

The **shape** of something is the line around the edge. A circle is a round **shape**. A square is a **shape** with four sides.

share

To **share** is to give away part of something. I **shared** my sweets with my brother. We had five sweets each.

sharp

Sharp things cut and scratch. Knives and needles are **sharp**.

sheep

A **sheep** is an animal that is covered with wool. You can see **sheep** on a farm.

bread

cold meat & cheese

meat

moustache

cheese

magazine

mone

Shopping

a b c d e f g h i j k l m

sheet

A **sheet** is a large piece of cloth that you put on a bed.

shelf

A **shelf** is a flat piece of wood or metal that sticks out from a wall. You can put things on **shelves**.

shell

A **shell** is a hard outside cover. Eggs and nuts have **shells**. Snails and some other animals have **shells**.

shine

To **shine** is to give light. The sun **shines**.

ship

A **ship** is a large boat.

shirt

You wear a **shirt** on the top half of your body. **Shirts** are usually made of thin cloth and have buttons down the front.

shoe

We wear **shoes** on our feet. **Shoes** are made of leather or plastic.

shoot

To **shoot** is to send a bullet or an arrow towards something or somebody. My uncle uses his gun to **shoot** birds.

shop

A **shop** is a place where you can buy things.

short

Short means small from end to end or from top to bottom.

shoulder

Your arm is joined to your body at your **shoulder**.

shout

When you **shout** you speak very loudly. I **shouted** to my friend at the other end of the field.

fruit & vegetables

banana

lemon

carrot

milk

bread

show

To **show** is to let people see something. My sister **showed** me her new coat.

shut

Shut is the opposite of open. **Shut** the gate so that the dog can't get out.

side

The **side** of something is the part by the edge. We moved the chairs to the **side** of the room so that we could dance in the middle.

sign

A **sign** tells you something. The **sign** EXIT shows us the way out. The **sign** = means 'equals'.

silver

Silver is a shiny white metal. Things that are made of **silver** cost a lot of money.

sing

To **sing** is to make music with your voice. People **sing** songs. Birds also **sing**.

sink

To **sink** is to go down. If you drop a stone into water, it will **sink** to the bottom.

sister

Mr and Mrs Smith have two children, Jane and Paul. Jane is Paul's **sister**. Do you have a **sister**?

sit

To **sit** is to rest on your bottom. You can **sit** on a chair or on the floor.

six

Six is the number that comes after five. Here are **six** pens.

size

The **size** of something is how big it is.

skate

When you **skate** you wear special shoes to help you slide along. Roller **skates** have wheels on the bottom. You wear ice **skates** to **skate** on ice.

skeleton

A **skeleton** is all the bones of a body.

skin

Your **skin** is the soft outside cover of your body.

skirt

A **skirt** is a piece of clothing that hangs down from the waist. Girls and women wear **skirts**.

sky

The **sky** is the space above the earth. The **sky** is blue on a sunny day.

sleep

To **sleep** is to rest with your eyes closed. You **sleep** in a bed at night.

slide

To **slide** is to move along smoothly. The children are playing on the **slide** in the park. Mark is **sliding** down.

slow

Something that is **slow** takes a long time. **Slow** is the opposite of fast.

small

Small is the opposite of large. These shoes are too **small**, I can't get my feet into them.

smell

You **smell** with your nose. Most flowers **smell** nice. Rotten food has a nasty **smell**.

smile

People **smile** when they are happy. When you **smile**, the ends of your mouth move upwards.

smoke

Smoke is a dark cloud that comes from fire.

smooth

Smooth means not rough. A **smooth** surface has no lumps in it.

snail

A **snail** is a small animal that has a hard shell. **Snails** move very slowly.

snake

A **snake** is an animal with a long thin body and no legs.

sneeze

A **sneeze** is a sudden noise that you make through your nose and mouth. We **sneeze** when we have a cold.

snow

Snow is cold and white. **Snow** falls from the sky in winter. You can build a snowman and make snowballs with **snow**.

soap

Soap makes things clean. We wash ourselves with **soap** and water.

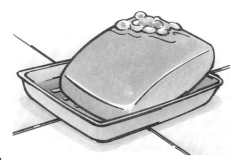

sock

You wear a **sock** on your foot, inside your shoe.

soft

Soft means not hard. A pillow is **soft**. You can make **soft** clay into different shapes.

son

A boy is the **son** of his father and mother.

song

A **song** has words and music. We sing **songs**. Do you know any **songs**?

sorry

You say **sorry** when you have done something wrong. I'm **sorry** I forgot to post your letter. I wish I hadn't forgotten, I feel bad about it.

sound

A **sound** is something that you hear.

space

A **space** is an empty place. When we write, we leave **spaces** between the words.
   Space is all around the earth and the stars. Astronauts travel in **space**.

spade

A **spade** is a tool that is used for digging.

speak

When you **speak**, you use your voice to make words. You're **speaking** too quietly, I can't hear you.

special

Something that is **special** is different from ordinary things. My mother made a **special** cake for my birthday.

spell

To **spell** is to use the right letters to make a word. How do you **spell** your name?

spend

We **spend** money when we buy something. We **spend** time when we do something.

spider

A **spider** is a small animal with eight legs. **Spiders** spin webs to catch insects.

spoon

We use a **spoon** to eat soup or ice cream. The round end of a **spoon** is shaped to hold food or liquid.

spot

A **spot** is a small round mark. This skirt is blue with white **spots**.

square

A **square** is a shape with four sides. All the sides of a **square** are the same length.

squirrel

A **squirrel** is an animal with a big bushy tail. **Squirrels** live in trees.

stairs

Stairs are steps inside a building. We climb up the **stairs** to get to the floor above.

stamp

A **stamp** is a small piece of paper. Before you post a letter, you must buy a **stamp** and stick it on the envelope.

splash

When something falls into water, it makes a **splash**. I jumped into the bath and **splashed** water all over the floor.

spring

Spring is the season between winter and summer. In **spring** the plants begin to grow.

stand

To **stand** is to stay still on your feet. There were no seats left, so we had to **stand**.

a b c d e f g h i j k l m

star

A **star** is a bright light that you can see in the sky at night. **Stars** are very far away from the earth.

start

To **start** means to begin. When you read a book, you **start** on the first page.

station

Trains stop at a **station**.

stay

If something **stays**, it does not move. My brother went to the party, but I **stayed** at home.

steal

When people **steal**, they take something that does not belong to them. Don't leave your bike in the road, somebody might **steal** it.

steam

When water boils it turns into **steam**. A cloud of **steam** came out of the kettle.

step

You take a **step** when you move your foot to walk or run or dance.

Steps are used to go up to a higher place or down to a lower place.

stick

A **stick** is a long thin piece of wood.

To **stick** is to join things together with glue. I'm going to **stick** these photographs in my album.

sting

To **sting** is to hurt. The salt water made my cut knee **sting**. Bees and wasps can **sting** you.

stitch

You make **stitches** with a needle and thread when you sew. **Stitches** hold our clothes together.

stone

A **stone** is a small hard lump of rock.

stool

A **stool** is a seat without a back.

stop

When something **stops**, it does not move any more. The train **stopped** at the station. If you **stop** doing something, you do not do it any more. The children **stopped** talking when the teacher came in.

storm

A **storm** is very bad weather. There is strong wind and heavy rain and there may be thunder and lightning in a **storm**.

story

You can read a **story** or tell a **story**. My sister wrote a **story** about an elephant who ran away from the circus and had lots of adventures.

straight

Something that is **straight** has no bends or curves. I use my ruler to draw a **straight** line.

stranger

A **stranger** is somebody you do not know. My mother told me not to speak to **strangers**.

street

A **street** is a road in the middle of a town or city.

stretch

To **stretch** is to make something longer. Elastic **stretches** when you pull it.

string

String is very thick thread. We use **string** to tie things up.

n o p q r **s** t u v w x y z

stripe

A **stripe** is a narrow band of colour. The balloon is green with a white **stripe**.

strong

A **strong** person can lift heavy things. My uncle pushed the car out of the ditch. He is very **strong**.

submarine

A **submarine** is a boat that travels under the water.

sugar

Sugar is a sweet food. Cakes and biscuits have **sugar** in them.

summer

Summer is the season between spring and autumn. **Summer** is the hottest time of the year.

sun

The **sun** is very bright and hot. It gives us light and heat.

Sunday

Sunday is one of the days of the week. **Sunday** comes after Saturday and before Monday.

supermarket

A **supermarket** is a big shop that sells food and other things. In a **supermarket** you take what you want and pay for it all at the end.

surprise

A **surprise** is something that you do not expect. I was **surprised** to see Robert at the park, I thought he had gone to the seaside.

swallow

When you **swallow** food or drink, it goes down your throat from your mouth to your stomach.

sweep

To **sweep** is to clean something with a brush. My father asked me to **sweep** up the leaves in the garden.

sweet

Chocolate and sugar and fruit and cakes are **sweet**. **Sweets** are small **sweet** things that are nice to eat.

swim

To **swim** is to use our arms and legs to move through water. Can you **swim**?

swing

When something **swings**, one end stays still and the other end moves from side to side. The children are playing on the **swings** in the park. They are **swinging** backwards and forwards.

t

table

A **table** is a piece of furniture with a flat top.

tail

A **tail** is at the end of an animal's body. Our dog wags his **tail** when he's happy.

take

When you **take** something, you pick it up and carry it with you. Don't forget to **take** your books back to the library.

talk

To **talk** is to speak to somebody. Peter is **talking** to his friend on the telephone.

tall

Tall means large from top to bottom. Giraffes are very **tall** animals.

tame

A **tame** animal is friendly to people. Pets are **tame**.

tap

If you want water, you turn on the **tap**. Hot water comes out of this **tap** and cold water comes out of that one.

taste

When you **taste** something, you eat a bit of it to see what it is like. This ice cream **tastes** of strawberries.

taxi

A **taxi** is a car that you pay to travel in.

tea

Tea is a hot drink.
   Tea is also a meal that we eat in the afternoon.

teach

To **teach** is to show somebody how to do something. My brother is **teaching** me how to swim.

teacher

Your **teacher** helps you to learn and understand things at school.

team

A **team** is a group of people who work or play together. The girls' **team** beat the boys' **team** in the netball match.

tear

A **tear** is a drop of water that comes out of your eye when you cry.
   If you **tear** paper or cloth, you make a hole in it or break it into pieces.

tease

When people **tease** you, they laugh at you and make you sad or angry.

telephone

We use a **telephone** to talk to somebody who is far away. A **telephone** is sometimes called a phone.

television

A **television** brings moving pictures and sounds into our house. What is your favourite **television** programme?

tell

To **tell** is to talk about something. **Tell** me about your holidays.

temperature

Temperature tells us how hot or cold something is. You sometimes have a high **temperature** when you are ill.

ten

Ten is the number that comes after nine. Here are **ten** children.

tent

A **tent** is like a small house made of cloth. You go to see a circus in a big tent.

test

To **test** is to try something to see if it works.

A **test** is also a number of questions to find out how much you know.

thank

We **thank** people who have done something for us or who have given us something. **Thank** you for mending my model train. I said '**Thank** you' for the present.

thermometer

You use a **thermometer** to find out the temperature. The **thermometer** on the wall tells us how warm the room is.

thick

Thick means wide from one side to the other. A **thick** book has a lot of pages.

thin

Thin is the opposite of thick. A piece of paper is **thin**.

think

When you **think**, you use your mind to work something out or to picture something. I was **thinking** about our new house. Can you **think** of the answer?

thirsty

If you are **thirsty**, you want a drink.

three

Three is the number that comes after two. Here are **three** kittens.

through

When you go **through** something, you go inside it from one side to the other. The train is going **through** the tunnel.

throw

To **throw** is to make something move through the air. **Throw** the ball to Jennifer.

thumb

We have a **thumb** on each hand. Your **thumb** is shorter and fatter than your fingers.

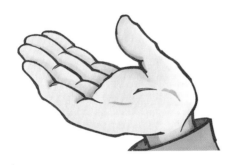

thunder

Thunder is a loud noise in the sky during a storm. **Thunder** comes after lightning.

Thursday

Thursday is one of the days of the week. **Thursday** comes after Wednesday and before Friday.

ticket

A **ticket** is a small piece of paper or cardboard. A **ticket** shows that you have paid to travel on a bus or train. You have to buy a **ticket** to go into the cinema.

tidy

When we **tidy** a room, we put everything in its place. Your desk is not very **tidy**, there are books and pens and papers all over the place.

tie

To **tie** is to fasten something with a knot. I

tied up the parcel with string. **Tie** one end of the rope to the boat and the other end to a post.

tiger

A **tiger** is a wild animal with stripes on its fur. You can see **tigers** at the zoo.

tight

Something that is **tight** fits very closely. These trousers are too **tight**. They are not big enough for me.

time

The **time** tells us when or how long. What **time** do you go to bed? It takes a long **time** to count to a thousand.

timetable

A **timetable** shows you what time something will happen. I looked at the **timetable** to find when the next train would come.

tiny

Tiny means very small.

tired

When you are **tired**, you need to rest. We were very **tired** after our long walk.

tissue

Tissue is soft thin paper. A **tissue** is a paper handkerchief.

toast

Toast is a piece of bread that has been cooked. **Toast** is brown and hard on both sides.

today

Today is this day. Yesterday was Tuesday, **today** is Wednesday, tomorrow will be Thursday.

toe

Our **toes** are at the ends of our feet. We have five **toes** on each foot.

tomato

A **tomato** is a red fruit. We eat **tomatoes** with cheese or meat or in a salad.

tomorrow

Tomorrow is the day after today.

You travel on a train from a railway station.

a b c d e f g h i j k l m

tongue

Your **tongue** is inside your mouth. It is soft and flat. Your **tongue** helps you to speak and to taste.

tool

Tools help people to work. A spade is a **tool**, so is a hammer.

tooth

A **tooth** is hard and white.
You have two rows of **teeth** inside your mouth.

top

The **top** is the highest part of something. We climbed up to the **top** of the hill.

touch

To **touch** is to put your finger or your hand on something. Can you **touch** your toes without bending your knees?

towel

A **towel** is a piece of soft cloth. We dry ourselves with a **towel**.

town

A **town** is a place with many roads and houses. People live and work in a **town**.

toy

A **toy** is something to play with. Dolls and games and model cars are **toys**.

track

A **track** is the rails that a train moves on.

tractor

A **tractor** is used to pull heavy things across a field or along the road.

traffic

Traffic is all the cars and trucks and vans and buses on the road. There is a lot of **traffic** on the motorway today.

train

A **train** carries people or things on a railway. A **train** is pulled by an engine.

telephone

taxi

travel

To **travel** is to go from one place to another.

treasure

Treasure is gold and silver and jewellery that is worth a lot of money. The **treasure** is hidden somewhere on this island.

tree

A **tree** is a large plant. Wood comes from **trees**.

triangle

A **triangle** is a shape with three sides and three corners.

trick

I played a **trick** on my sister. I hid her library books and she thought she had lost them. Our uncle did a magic **trick**, he made my watch disappear.

trolley

A **trolley** has wheels. You can use a **trolley** to help you move heavy things. At the supermarket we put all the things we want to buy in our **trolley**.

trouble

You will be in **trouble** if somebody catches you doing something wrong. My naughty brother is always getting into **trouble**.

trousers

Trousers are clothes. **Trousers** cover your legs and your body up to your waist.

truck

A **truck** carries heavy things along the road. A **truck** is bigger than a van.

true

If something is **true**, it really happened. Our grandfather told us a **true** story about his adventures at sea. Is it **true** that bats are blind?

trumpet

A **trumpet** is a musical instrument that is made of metal. You play a **trumpet** by blowing into it.

try

When you **try**, you find out if you can do something. I **tried** to lift the rock, but it was too heavy. I will **try** to write more neatly.

Tuesday

Tuesday is one of the days of the week. **Tuesday** comes after Monday and before Wednesday.

tunnel

A **tunnel** is a long hole through a hill or under the ground.

turn

To **turn** is to go round. Wheels **turn**. When you **turn**, you look or go a different way. **Turn** left at the end of the road.

twelve

Twelve is the number that comes after eleven. Here are **twelve** birds.

twin

Twins are two people who were born on the same day and who have the same mother and father. **Twins** often look like each other.

two

Two is the number that comes after one. There are **two** houses in this picture.

tyre

A **tyre** is a rubber ring on the wheel of a car or a bicycle. **Tyres** are filled with air.

TRUE OR FALSE

'A banana is an animal.' True or false? It's false – a banana is not an animal, it's a fruit.

'You wear shoes on your feet.' True or false? It's true.

Here are some more. Are they true or false? You can find all the answers in this dictionary.

1 An insect has five legs.
2 Camels live in the desert.
3 An onion is a vegetable.
4 A kitten is a young dog.
5 Tuesday is the day after Monday.
6 Your hand is at the end of your leg.
7 New means old.
8 Winter is the hottest time of the year.
9 A prince is the son of a king or queen.
10 Lemons are yellow.

Answers on page 96

n o p q r s t u v w x y z

ugly

Ugly means not pretty. An **ugly** person is not nice to look at.

umbrella

You hold an **umbrella** over your head when it is raining. The **umbrella** keeps you dry.

uncle

Your **uncle** is your mother's brother or your father's brother.

under

Under means below. The puppy hid **under** the bed.

understand

To **understand** is to know what something means. I didn't **understand** what the French children were saying.

uniform

If you wear a **uniform**, you wear the same clothes as people you are with. Policemen and nurses wear **uniforms**. So do Scouts and Guides. Some children wear a school **uniform**.

untidy

Untidy is the opposite of tidy. My sister's bedroom is always **untidy**, she never puts her clothes or her toys away.

use

We **use** something to do something. We **use** a spade to dig. We **use** a pen to write.

---

van

A **van** carries things along the road. A **van** is smaller than a truck.

vase

You can put flowers in a **vase**. You must put water in the **vase** before you put the flowers in.

vegetable

A **vegetable** is part of a plant that we can eat. Cabbages, carrots, peas and potatoes are all **vegetables**.

view

A **view** is what you can see. You get a good **view** of the town from the top of this building.

village

A **village** is a small town in the country.

violin

A **violin** is a musical instrument. You play a **violin** by pulling the bow across the strings.

visit

To **visit** is to go and see a person or a place. I **visited** my aunt in hospital.

voice

You use your **voice** to speak or sing. Our teacher always talks in a loud **voice**.

volcano

A **volcano** is a mountain that explodes. Hot liquid comes out of a hole at the top of the **volcano**.

waist

Your **waist** is in the middle of your body. You can wear a belt around your **waist**.

wait

If you **wait**, you do not do something straight away. **Wait** for me! Stay where you are until I get there.

wake

To **wake** is to stop sleeping. I always **wake** up at seven o'clock.

walk

To **walk** is to move along using your legs.

wall

A **wall** is made of bricks. **Walls** are the sides of a house. There is a low **wall** at the end of our garden.

wand

A **wand** is a stick that is used for magic. The fairy is waving her magic **wand**.

want

If you **want** something, you would like to have it. I **want** a computer. What do you **want** to do this afternoon?

war

When two countries fight each other, they have a **war**.

warm

Warm is between hot and cold. We wear gloves to keep our hands **warm**.

wash

To **wash** is to make something clean. I **washed** my face with soap and water.

waste

If you **waste** something, you do not use it well. Don't leave the light on, you're **wasting** electricity.

watch

A **watch** shows us the time. You can wear a **watch** around your wrist.
    To **watch** is to look at something for a time. I like **watching** television.

water

Water is a clear liquid. You can drink cold **water**. We wash with hot **water**. Rain is **water**. The sea is **water**.

wave

To **wave** is to move your hand or something else from side to side. I **waved** to my friend across the street.

weak

Weak is the opposite of strong. This fence is **weak**, it will break if you lean on it.

wear

You **wear** clothes on your body.

weather

The **weather** is how hot or cold and wet or dry it is outside. Rain, snow, wind and sunshine are all kinds of **weather**.

web

A **web** is a lot of thin threads that cross over each other. A spider spins a **web**.

wedding

A man and a woman get married at a **wedding**. I wore my new dress at my aunt's **wedding**.

Wednesday

Wednesday is one of the days of the week. **Wednesday** comes after Tuesday and before Thursday.

week

A **week** is seven days. There are 52 **weeks** in a year.

In fairyland

a b c d e f g h i j k l m

weigh

When you **weigh** something, you find out how heavy it is.

wet

Water makes things **wet**. **Wet** is the opposite of dry.

whale

A **whale** is a very big animal that lives in the sea.

wheel

A **wheel** is round. **Wheels** help things to move along. A bicycle has two **wheels**.

web

castle

wheel

whisper

To **whisper** is to speak very quietly. I **whispered** the answer to David because I didn't want everybody else to hear.

whistle

A **whistle** makes a high sound. The teacher blew her **whistle** and the children stood still. You can also **whistle** by blowing through your lips.

white

White is the colour of snow. Milk also is **white**.

whole

Whole means all. I have eaten the **whole** cake, there is none left.

wide

Wide means big from side to side. The river was too **wide** to jump, we had to swim across.

wife

A man's **wife** is the woman he is married to. My mother is my father's **wife**.

wild

A **wild** animal is not tame. A **wild** flower does not grow in a garden.

win

To **win** is to be better than everybody else. Judy will **win** the race if she runs faster than all the other children.

wind

Wind is moving air. The **wind** blew my hat off.

window

A **window** is a piece of glass in the side of a house or a car. You can look out through a **window**.

wing

Birds and some insects have **wings**. They use their **wings** to fly. Aeroplanes also have **wings**.

winter

Winter is the season between autumn and spring. **Winter** is the coldest time of the year.

wish

To **wish** is to want something. I **wish** I could drive a car.

woman

A **woman** is a female adult. Your mother and your aunt are **women**.

wood

Wood comes from trees. Some tables and chairs are made of **wood**.

word

A **word** is a group of letters that means something. Books are full of **words**.

work

To **work** is to do something. When you are **working**, you are not resting or playing. My father **works** in a factory.

world

The **world** is where everybody lives. There are many different countries in the **world**.

worm

A **worm** is a long thin animal that lives in the ground. Birds eat **worms**.

wrap

To **wrap** is to cover something by putting paper or cloth around it. I **wrapped** up the present in fancy paper.

wrist

Your hand is joined to your arm at your **wrist**.

write

To **write** is to put words on paper. I used my new pen to **write** a letter to my cousin.

wrong

Wrong means not right. You've given me the **wrong** coat, this is Steven's coat.

a b c d e f g h i j k l m

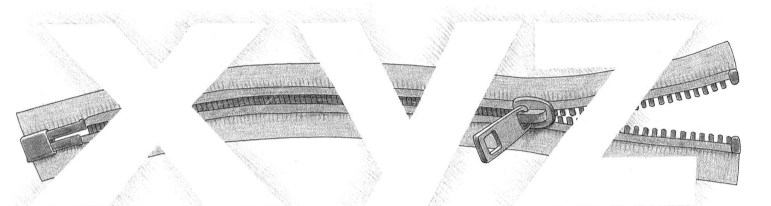

x-ray

An **x-ray** is a photograph that shows the bones inside your body. The doctor took an **x-ray** of my arm to see if I had broken it.

xylophone

A **xylophone** is a musical instrument. You play a **xylophone** by hitting the strips of wood or metal with small hammers.

yacht

A **yacht** is a boat with sails.

yawn

When you **yawn**, you open your mouth wide. We **yawn** when we are tired or bored.

year

A **year** is twelve months, 52 weeks, or 365 days. My sister is eight **years** old.

yellow

Yellow is the colour of a ripe banana.

yesterday

Yesterday is the day before today.

young

Young means not old. A child is a **young** person. A kitten is a **young** cat.

yo-yo

A **yo-yo** is a round toy on a string. You can make the **yo-yo** roll up and down the string.

zebra

A **zebra** is an animal like a horse with black and white stripes.

zero

Zero means nothing. The number 300 is written with a three and two **zeros**.

zip

A **zip** is used to fasten skirts and trousers and other clothes.

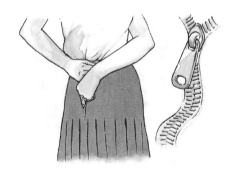

zoo

A **zoo** is a place where you can see lots of wild animals. Some animals live in cages at the **zoo**.